D0857158

simply bread

METRO BOOKS
New York

An Imprint of Sterling Publishing
387 Park Avenue South
New York, NY 10016

METRO BOOKS and the distinctive Metro Books logo are trademarks of Sterling Publishing Co., Inc

Copyright © 2013 Pulp Media Limited

This 2013 edition published by Metro Books by arrangement with Pulp Media Limited

All rights reserved. No part of this publication may be reproduced, stored in a retrieval system,
or transmitted, in any form or by any means, electronic, mechanical, photocopying, recording, or otherwise,
without prior written permission from the publishers and copyright holder.

Written by Wendy Sweetser
Additional writing by Sara Bang-Melchior
Project Editors: Julia Aitken and Jill Steed
Translation of Swedish recipes: Deborah Larsson
Art Director: Geoff Borin
Food styling in Ian Garlick's photographs: Wendy Sweetser
Publisher: James Tavendale

Every effort has been made to credit photographers and copyright-holders. If any have been
overlooked, Pulp Media will be pleased to make the necessary corrections in subsequent editions
and on their website www.pulp.me.com

ISBN: 978-1-4351-4547-4

For information about custom editions, special sales, and premium and corporate purchases,
please contact Sterling Special Sales at 800-805-5489 or specialsales@sterlingpublishing.com

Printed in China

10 9 8 7 6 5 4 3 2 1

www.sterlingpublishing.com

simply bread

SIMPLE RECIPES FOR HOMEMADE LOAVES, ROLLS AND FLATBREADS

WENDY SWEETSER AND SARA BANG-MELCHIOR

METRO BOOKS
New York

"Good **bread** is the most fundamentally satisfying of all foods; and good bread with **fresh** butter, the greatest of feasts."

James Beard

contents

introduction

One of life's pleasures…

It's said that if you're trying to sell your house, a loaf of bread baking in the oven
when prospective buyers call is one of the surest ways to convince them to make
an offer. And certainly there are few things more enticing than the smell of newly
baked bread, its warm aroma drifting to every room and somehow turning the
house into a home.

The whole process of making your own bread is curiously rewarding and
comforting in a way that no other type of cooking can quite match. Robust stews,
slow-cooked pot roasts or a batch of chocolate-chip cookies all smell good in the
oven but none of them can compete with the pleasure a well-made loaf brings
both to the baker and those lucky enough to share it.

Bread-making is also a great way to relax in an ever-crazier world. It's true
that loaves raised with chemical agents like baking powder or baking soda are
quick and easy to make and can be baked as soon as the ingredients are mixed
but doughs leavened with yeast require time and patience. Don't be tempted to
make your yeast dough rise more quickly by leaving it in a hot place; it needs an
environment that's warm and dry and enough time to rise.

Bread is a staple part of the diet of many countries around the world but
while we in the West tend to take it for granted when making our breakfast toast
or lunchtime sandwich, other cultures revere it, baking special loaves to mark
religious festivals and ceremonial occasions. In Russia kulich is baked at Easter
to be blessed by the priest at the local Orthodox church, fougasse celebrates

Christmas Eve in France, while Jewish communities mark Shabbat by baking braided challah loaves.

So what has made bread such an iconic part of our lives for so long? One reason for its lasting attraction must be the simplicity of the ingredients needed to produce a basic loaf – flour, salt, water and a raising agent – that haven't changed since the time of the Ancient Egyptians. With these four basic items, different cultures have adapted bread recipes using local produce to make loaves suited to their climate and lifestyle. Dark rye flour is commonly used in the cool countries of Scandinavia to bake dark, dense loaves with a flavor not dissimilar to sourdough, while warmer parts of the world such as the countries that border the Mediterranean and those in southeast Asia, use lighter wheat flours to bake soft-textured loaves like the Italian focaccia, Greek pita and Indian naan.

In this book you'll find recipes for breads for all occasions, from simple rolls and everyday loaves to more exotic treats like flatbreads, festive breads and loaves flavored with dried fruits, nuts, spices, herbs and even pumpkin. We've also included recipes made with gluten-free flours, buckwheat flour and bran so family and friends who need to omit gluten from their diet don't miss out when everyone else is breaking bread.

So, get into the kitchen, roll up your sleeves and let's get baking!

Wendy Sweetser

getting started

which flour?

The better the flour you buy to make your bread, the better the texture and flavor of your loaf will be.

To produce flour, cereal grains have to be ground to separate the three parts of the grain – the bran, the endosperm and the germ. Bran is the dark outer husk of the kernel and contains fiber and minerals. It surrounds the endosperm, which provides protein and starch, while the germ is rich in oil and nutrients.

Wheat is the cereal most commonly used for making bread flour but flours made with other cereals are also available, each adding its own characteristic flavor.

WHEAT FLOUR – when making bread look for plain or all-purpose flour labelled 'strong' or 'bread' flour. 'Strong' means the flour has been made from hard wheat that has a high proportion of protein to starch, the protein determining the amount of gluten that can be developed when the dough is kneaded. Gluten stretches and expands the dough giving the baked loaf a light-textured crumb.

Wheat flour can be white or whole wheat, the latter being coarser and producing a loaf with a rougher texture but a nuttier, fuller flavor.

SPELT FLOUR is made from finely milled spelt grains, a cereal widely cultivated since ancient times. It belongs to the same family as wheat but is higher in vitamins, minerals, proteins and carbohydrates. Once widely grown in Continental Europe, spelt has enjoyed a revival in recent times due to its nutritional benefits being recognized.

The flour is pale grayish-yellow, has a gritty texture and gives a nutty, quite sweet flavor to a loaf. The protein is easier to digest so although spelt flour is not suitable for a gluten-free diet, it may be tolerated by some people with an allergy to common wheat. It it can replace all purpose flour in recipes.

MANITOBA CREAM, sometimes just called Canadian flour, has an extra-high protein content (even higher than strong bread flour) and is the professional baker's favorite. It is used to great advantage in a variety of recipes and we recommend it in this book. It can be bought from specialist retailers or online. Sir Lancelot flour is a good equivalent.

RYE FLOUR was once a staple cereal in northern, eastern and central Europe as the climate was too cold and the soil too poor to grow wheat. Gray-brown in color and low in protein, it makes well-flavored loaves that have a dark, dense, chewy texture. For a lighter loaf, the rye flour can be mixed with wheat flour. A high proportion of rye flour in a dough works best if a sourdough starter is used.

ITALIAN '00' FLOUR – the Italians grade their flour according to how finely ground it is with '00' being suitable for everyday bread recipes. Lower in protein than strong bread flour, it produces a crisper crust.

GLUTEN-FREE FLOUR is designed for baking loaves than can be eaten by anyone who must avoid gluten. As well as proprietary brands of gluten-free flour available in supermarkets, flours made from grains other than wheat such as corn, chickpeas, quinoa, tapioca, chestnut and buckwheat, and vegetable flours like potato, are also gluten-free. Lack of gluten means a bread dough made with one of these flours has the texture of a batter rather than a conventional dough and needs baking powder to raise it, but make sure to use baking powder labeled 'gluten-free'.

raising agents

YEAST is the most common raising agent used to leaven bread. It is available as fresh bakers' yeast, active dry yeast and quick-rise (also known as instant) dried yeast. As quick-rise yeast is the most widely available in supermarkets and food shops, we've used that for the recipes in this book that but you can substitute fresh yeast or active dry yeast if you prefer as the three types are interchangeable when making bread dough as long as a few simple rules are followed.

Quick-rise or instant dried yeast is widely available in supermarkets either in jars or packaged in small envelopes. Twice as strong as fresh yeast – 1½–2 tsp is equivalent to ½ oz fresh yeast – it needs to be sprinkled over the dry flour and mixed in before any liquid is added.

Bakers' fresh yeast is available from artisanal bakers, whole-food stores and some larger supermarkets' refrigerated section and is sold in grayish-brown, putty-like blocks. It can be stored in the fridge for up to 2 weeks or can be divided up into ½ oz portions, wrapped tightly and frozen. Defrost the yeast in the fridge until it just softens but don't leave it for too long or it will dissolve into a sticky brown liquid.

When using fresh yeast to make plain bread dough, allow ½ oz to 4 cups (1 lb 2 oz) flour and, if adapting a recipe that uses dried yeast, use double the quantity of fresh yeast.

Before adding fresh yeast to flour, crumble it into a little of the warm liquid specified in the recipe and set it aside until a thick froth forms on the surface. The froth shows the yeast is active and it can then be poured into the flour followed by the other ingredients.

Active dry yeast needs to be mixed with water and sugar and left until frothy before being added to flour. It has the same strength as quick-rise or instant dried yeast.

SOURDOUGH STARTERS make breads that have a good flavor and rise well. These naturally fermented starters use wild yeasts present in the air and on grains and can be made using white, whole wheat or rye flour plus water. Sourdough starters have been used for thousands of year and are made without the addition of commercial yeast.

BAKING POWDER can be used to leaven quick breads such as Irish soda bread and gluten-free breads. Standard and gluten-free baking powders are available.

FAT AND SALT Both of these give bread dough elasticity and add flavor. Butter adds richness and needs to be at room temperature so it is soft enough to be easily incorporated into the dough.

While salt definitely improves the flavor of a baked loaf, if you or anyone you are baking for needs to watch the level of sodium in their diet, the amount of salt given in the recipes in this book can be reduced or omitted.

TEMPERATURE is crucial to the fermentation process so getting it right will determine whether your dough rises or remains a tight, heavy ball.

The liquid added to the flour can be water or milk but it should be no hotter than tepid – around blood heat, 98.4 F. The easiest way to check this is to dip a finger in the liquid and it should feel very slightly warm. Too hot and you'll kill the yeast, too cold and the leavening process will be slowed or even stopped.

Once you've made your dough, place it in an oiled bowl and cover the bowl tightly with plastic wrap or slide the bowl into a large plastic bag and seal it tightly. Leave the dough in a warm place that's between 68°F and 95°F (depending on how quickly you want the dough to rise) until it has doubled in size.

Doughs that rise slowly at a lower temperature generally have a better texture and flavor and better keeping qualities than quickly risen doughs. If you're not in a hurry, the dough can be left to rise overnight in the fridge or in a cold room.

getting the basics right

KNEADING

Dough must be kneaded to work the gluten in the flour so the dough becomes smooth and elastic and rises properly. This can be done by hand on a lightly floured board or in an electric stand mixer with a dough hook fitted.

If kneading by hand, put the dough on a lightly floured surface and stretch and pull it vigorously as you work it to develop the gluten, which along with the gas bubbles the yeast produces, will make the dough rise.

To knead the dough, use the heel of your hand to push it away from you and then fold it back towards you to make a ball, turning the dough as you go. You'll need to do this for about 10 minutes to get the dough to the right spongy texture.

If using an electric food mixer, follow the manufacturer's instructions, don't overfill the bowl and switch the machine to low speed, working the dough for about 5 minutes.

Once the dough has risen, punch it down with your fist and knead it again – this time by hand – for 1–2 minutes to burst any air bubbles in it.

RISING

After the first kneading, shape the dough into a ball, place it in a lightly oiled bowl, cover the bowl tightly and leave it in a warm place (see TEMPERATURE on page 23) until it has doubled in size. Once the dough begins to rise, check it regularly as if it is left to rise too much, the loaf could collapse when it goes in the oven.

Rich, sweet, yeasted doughs will take longer to rise than plain bread doughs.

SHAPING

Once the dough has risen, knock it down and knead briefly to make it smooth. Shape your dough into a ball, a braid, a rectangular loaf or individual rolls or buns as you wish and place in a greased pan or on a greased baking sheet.

PROVING

Cover the shaped dough loosely with cling film – oil the film lightly this time to stop the dough sticking to it as it rises – and leave it in a warm place until it doubles in size. This second rising will help ensure the crumb of the baked bread has a more even texture than if it were only risen once.

BAKING

The top of your loaf can be glazed by brushing it with beaten egg or milk and sprinkling it with poppy seeds or sesame seeds, if you like. Alternatively, it can be left plain or lightly dusted with flour.

Bread needs to go into a hot oven so the yeast is killed off quickly. Crusty loaves need to be baked at a higher temperature than ones with a soft crust.

To test if a loaf is cooked, remove it from the oven and tap the base of it – it should sound hollow rather than dense. And remember it's better to over-bake rather than under-bake bread.

If the loaf is baked in a pan, protect your hands with oven mitts and turn the loaf out of the pan so you can tap the base. If it's not ready, return the loaf to the pan and continue baking. If it's done and you want to crisp the underneath and sides, lay the loaf on its side on a baking sheet and return it to the oven for 5–10 minutes.

making simple loaves

If you are new to baking bread, a good way to gain confidence is to start by making a basic white or whole wheat loaf. As long as you are careful not to kill the yeast by using liquid that is too hot and you get the feel of kneading dough by hand, you'll soon discover that breadmaking is not at all difficult. It can become addictive, though, and before long you'll be itching to experiment with some of the more challenging recipes in this book.

For these basic recipes we've included details on how to use both quick-rise dried yeast and fresh yeast.

basic white bread

MAKES: 1 large loaf

BAKING TIME: 35 minutes

5 cups (1½ lb) bread flour, plus extra if kneading by hand

1 tsp salt

1½ tsp quick-rise dried yeast OR ½ oz fresh yeast

1¾ cups warm water

⅓ cup oil, of your choice, plus extra for greasing

If using fresh yeast:

1 Crumble the yeast into a small bowl and stir in ¼ cup of the warm water until smooth. Set aside in a warm place until a thick froth appears on top of the liquid. Sift the flour and salt into a mixing bowl and mix in the yeast and the rest of the warm water and the oil. Work everything together with your hands to make a dough.

The rest of the recipe is the same for either type of yeast:

2 Knead the dough by hand on a floured surface for about 10 minutes or in an electric stand mixer with a dough hook fitted for 5 minutes on slow speed until the dough is smooth and elastic.

3 Place the dough in an oiled bowl, cover with plastic wrap and leave in a warm place for 1–1½ hours or until it has doubled in size.

variations

4 Remove the plastic wrap and punch the dough down with your fist. Transfer it to a floured surface and knead for 1–2 minutes by hand to remove any large air bubbles.

5 Shape the dough into a ball and lift it onto a lightly greased or non-stick baking sheet. Cover it with greased plastic wrap and leave in a warm place to rise for about 1 hour or until doubled in size.

6 Preheat the oven to 425°F. Uncover the loaf and cut several slashes across the top with a sharp, floured knife.

7 Bake for 35 minutes or until the loaf sounds hollow when tapped underneath. Transfer to a wire rack to cool.

WHOLE WHEAT BREAD

Follow the recipe for Basic White Bread but replace the bread flour with whole wheat bread flour. Depending on the flour you use, it may be necessary to add a little extra warm water if the dough is quite dry. Using 100% whole wheat flour makes a heavier dough and the baked loaf will have a closer-textured crumb so a good compromise is to replace just half the strong white flour with whole wheat flour.

RYE BREAD

Using all rye flour to make the dough will result in a heavy loaf so, for a lighter result, follow the recipe for Basic White Bread but replace just one quarter of the bread flour with rye flour.

how to make a sourdough starter

Using a sourdough starter to make a dough will give your baked loaf a moist texture and a deliciously sour flavor. It will also increase the length of time the loaf can be kept.

The principle behind sourdough is to capture and grow wild yeasts in the air and on flour so they produce carbon dioxide bubbles and lactic acid that add flavor to the dough and make it rise. Making a sourdough starter is not difficult – nature does most of the work for you – but it does take time as the starter needs a few days to become 'alive' and during this time you have to feed it.

Once this process is underway the starter is ready to be used but it will keep indefinitely if you look after it by feeding it every 5 days or so. Store the starter in the fridge in a plastic container or glass jar and bring it back to room temperature before using.

Feed it 6 hours before you want to make your bread and it should turn bubbly again. If you don't use your starter for a while it will separate into a dark liquid with a thicker paste below. Simply stir it up and feed it as before, unless it has a strong, unpleasant smell in which case it has to be thrown away.

Unbleached bread flour is most commonly used to make a sourdough starter but other flours such as whole wheat and rye are also suitable.

plain sourdough starter

DAY 1

¾ cup (3½ oz) unbleached bread flour

½ cup warm water (still mineral water is best or use filtered, boiled and cooled tap water)

FOR EACH FEEDING

¾ cup (3½ oz) unbleached bread flour

warm water (still mineral water or filtered, boiled and cooled tap water)

1 On day 1, put the flour in a small bowl and stir in the warm water. Cover the bowl with a damp kitchen towel and secure with an elastic, rather than using plastic wrap.

2 Leave the bowl somewhere that is free from drafts, dampening the towel again as necessary. After 2–4 days the paste should smell milky and slightly sour. If it smells bad and has patches of mold on it, you'll have to discard it and begin again.

3 Give your starter its first feed by adding another ¾ cup (3½ oz) flour and enough warm water to return it to a soft, sticky dough. Work the dough with a wooden spoon or your hand so plenty of air is incorporated into it. Re-cover the bowl with a damp kitchen towel and leave for 24 hours.

4 Stir the starter and spoon out and discard half of it. Add another ¾ cup (3½ oz) flour and more warm water to make a dough as before. Cover and leave for 12 hours.

5 By now the starter should be well and truly active and ready to use. Measure off the amount you need to make a loaf and keep the rest for the next time, continuing to feed the starter with flour and warm water as before. The starter should be bubbly and ready to use again after about 6–8 hours. If it doesn't look sufficiently active, you will need to halve it again and feed as before.

6 Keep the starter in the fridge and feed it every 5 days or so.

rye sourdough starter

DAY 1

2 cups (7 oz) rye flour

1¼ cups warm water

1 Tbsp liquid honey

DAY 3

2 cups (7 oz) rye flour

¾ cup warm water

AFTER THAT, FEED ONCE A
WEEK WITH:

¼ cup water

1–2 Tbsp rye flour

1 On day 1, mix the rye flour with the warm water and honey to make a firm mixture.

2 Store in a bowl covered with plastic wrap or a plastic container with a lid, filling the bowl only half full.

3 Leave the mixture to stand at room temperature for 2–3 days, stirring it once or twice a day. When it starts to bubble, becomes slightly acidic and smells sharp, it is time for the next step.

4 On day 3, or when the mixture bubbles, add the rye flour and warm water and leave it to stand for 24 hours after which time the sourdough is ready to use.

5 Feed the dough once a week with ¼ cup of water and 1–2 Tbsp rye flour.

bread rolls

Whether it's bagels to stuff with salmon and cream cheese or buns to pile high with burgers and relishes – or you just want something a bit more interesting than a hunk of yesterday's bread to serve with a bowl of soup – you'll find all the recipes you need in this chapter for both old favourites and new look rolls and small loaves.

mini seeded loaves

These small brown loaves with their topping of rolled oats can be eaten on their own with butter and jam or if you need a quick but satisfying lunch, serve them as an accompaniment to a bowl of thick, heart-warming soup.

MAKES: 12 mini loaves

BAKING TIME: 20 minutes

3 cups (12 oz) seeded white bread flour

¾ cup (4 oz) bread flour, plus extra for kneading

⅔ cup (3 oz) strong whole wheat bread flour

½ cup sunflower seeds

2 Tbsp onion seeds

1 Tbsp light muscovado sugar

2 tsp salt

1½ tsp quick-rise yeast

1 cup warm water

⅓ cup plain yogurt

4 tsp sunflower oil, plus extra for greasing

milk, for brushing

3 Tbsp rolled oats

1 Mix the three flours together in a bowl and stir in the sunflower and onion seeds, sugar, salt and yeast. Mix together the water, yogurt and sunflower oil and add to the dry ingredients, mixing to make a dough.

2 Draw the dough into a ball and knead lightly on a floured surface for a few minutes until you have a rough, slightly sticky ball. Transfer the dough to an oiled bowl, cover with plastic wrap and leave in a warm place for about 1 hour or until doubled in size.

3 Push the dough down with your fist, turn it out and knead by hand on a lightly floured surface for about 10 minutes or for 4–5 minutes in an electric mixer fitted with a dough hook. The dough will have lost its original stickiness and now be easier to work with.

4 Place 12 greased mini loaf pans on one large or two smaller baking sheets, divide the dough in half and then cut each half into six even-size pieces. Put a piece of dough into each loaf pan, brush with milk and scatter the oats on top. Cover the baking sheets with plastic wrap and leave in a warm place until doubled in size.

5 Preheat the oven to 375°F. Remove the plastic wrap and bake the loaves for 20 minutes or until they are golden, can be popped out of their pans easily and sound hollow when tapped on the bottom.

TIP If you don't have any mini loaf pans, the dough can be divided into 12, rolled into balls and baked as round or oval rolls. Let the rolls rise on a baking sheet and bake in the same way as for the mini loaves.

hamburger buns

Keep a batch of these in the freezer so they're ready to be split and toasted and filled with freshly grilled quarter pounders straight off the grill. Mini versions of the buns can be filled with small burgers or thin slices of grilled steak to make 'sliders,' the ideal finger food for a summer party.

MAKES: 10 buns

BAKING TIME: 10–12 minutes

FOR THE BURGER BUNS

3½ cups (1 lb 2 oz) bread flour, plus extra if kneading by hand

2 tsp quick-rise dried yeast

1 tsp granulated sugar

1 tsp salt

1¼ cups warm milk

2 Tbsp butter, melted

oil, for greasing

beaten egg, to glaze

sesame seeds, to sprinkle

TO SERVE

10 grilled burgers

20 lettuce leaves

4–5 tomatoes, sliced

10 cheese slices

Relish, ketchup, mustard, mayonnaise and/or dill pickles

1 Sift the flour into a bowl and stir in the yeast, sugar and salt. Beat together the milk and melted butter and pour into the dry ingredients. Mix to make a dough.

2 Turn out the dough onto a floured surface and knead by hand for 10 minutes or for 5 minutes in an electric stand mixer fitted with a dough hook until the dough is smooth and elastic.

3 Place the dough in an oiled bowl, cover with plastic wrap and leave in a warm place for about 1½ hours or until doubled in size.

4 Knock the dough down, knead again on a floured surface for 1–2 minutes then divide it into 10 even-size pieces. Roll each piece into a ball and press the tops to flatten.

5 Place the buns on a greased baking sheet, spacing them apart so they have room to rise, cover with a damp kitchen towel and leave in a warm place for 30–40 minutes or until the buns have doubled in size.

6 Preheat the oven to 425°F. Brush the tops of the buns with beaten egg to glaze and sprinkle with sesame seeds. Bake for 10–12 minutes or until golden on top.

7 Cool the buns on a wire rack. When ready to serve, split in half and toast the cut sides. Fill with burgers, lettuce, tomato and cheese slices and serve with your favorite fixings.

ciabatta

In Italian, 'ciabatta' means 'slipper' and these moist open-textured loaves with their floury crust came originally from the area of northern Italy around Lake Como. Today ciabatta, either as a single large loaf or as individual rolls, is popular around the world. A starter dough, called 'biga,' needs to be prepared the day before you want to make the main dough for the rolls, which are best eaten warm from the oven or within 24 hours.

MAKES: 12 ciabatta rolls

BAKING TIME: 15–20 minutes

FOR THE BIGA:

1¾ cups (9 oz) bread flour, plus extra for dusting

½ tsp quick-rise dried yeast

⅔ cup warm water

FOR THE DOUGH

1¼ cups warm water

1½ cups (10 oz) semolina flour

1½ cups (7 oz) strong white bread flour

1½ tsp quick-rise dried yeast

1½ tsp salt

4 Tbsp extra virgin olive oil

1 To make the biga, sift the flour into a mixing bowl and stir in the yeast. Gradually work the water into the dry ingredients to make a firm dough. Knead the dough on a board for 1–2 minutes then return it to the bowl, cover with plastic wrap and leave at room temperature for 12–24 hours during which time it will rise up then fall back again.

2 To make the dough, transfer the biga to the bowl of an electric stand mixer fitted with a dough hook and mix in the warm water on low speed to make a thick batter.

3 Mix together the semolina flour, bread flour and yeast, and add half of the flour mixture to the bowl. Continue mixing on low speed for 3–4 minutes or until the dough is very elastic. Cover the bowl with plastic wrap and leave to rise in a warm place for about 2 hours or until the dough has nearly tripled in size.

3 Add the olive oil, salt and remaining flour mixture and beat on low speed until the dough is smooth and stretchy. Cover the bowl as before and leave in a warm place to rise again for about 1½ hours or until doubled in size.

4 Transfer the dough to a board dusted with flour and, using a well-floured knife, divide it into 12 even-size pieces. Shape each piece into a rectangular n oblong or oval roll, divide the rolls between two greased baking sheets and dust liberally with flour.

5 Place each baking sheet in a large plastic bag, seal and leave the rolls to prove rise in a warm place for about 30 minutes or until they have almost doubled in size.

6 Preheat the oven to 450°°F. Uncover the rollsRemove the baking sheets from the plastic bags and bake for 15–20 minutes or until golden brown. Transfer to a wire rack to cool.

tomato, olive and rosemary pinwheels

The dough used to make these delicious Mediterranean-style rolls needs to be started the day before you want to bake them but, once made, the starter can be left in the fridge for up to 72 hours.

MAKES: about 12 pinwheels

BAKING TIME: 12–15 minutes

FOR THE STARTER

1¼ cups (5 oz) bread flour, plus extra for dusting

1½ tsp quick-rise yeast

½ tsp superfine sugar

⅔ cup warm water

FOR THE DOUGH

1 cup (5 oz) Italian '00' bread flour

1½ tsp quick-rise yeast

½ tsp salt

Scant ½ cup warm water

1 tsp olive oil

oil, for greasing

FOR THE FILLING

1 Tbsp olive oil

3 oz pitted black olives, chopped

3 oz sun-blushed tomatoes or sun-dried tomatoes, chopped

1 Tbsp finely chopped fresh rosemary leaves

1 To make the starter, sift the flour into a bowl and stir in the yeast and sugar. Add the warm water and mix well until you have a thick, smooth paste. Cover with plastic wrap and leave to rise for a minimum of 8 hours or preferably overnight.

2 To make the dough, mix together the '00' bread flour, yeast and salt and add to the starter with the warm water and olive oil. Transfer to the bowl of an electric mixer fitted with a dough hook and work the dough until it leaves the sides of the bowl – it will still be sticky but become firmer.

3 Put the dough to an oiled bowl, cover with plastic wrap and leave to rise for about 1½ hours or until doubled in size.

4 Knock the dough down, transfer it to a floured surface and press it out with your hands to a 12- x 6-inch rectangle.

5 To make the filling, smear the dough with the olive oil and scatter over the chopped olives, tomatoes and rosemary. Roll up from one long side like a jelly roll and cut into 1¼-inch slices with a floured sharp knife.

6 Divide the pinwheels between two greased and floured baking sheets, cover with a damp kitchen towel and leave to rise in a warm place for 15 minutes until puffy.

7 Preheat the oven to 425°F and bake the pinwheels for 12–15 minutes or until golden. Transfer to a wire rack to cool.

parker house rolls

Named after Boston's celebrated Parker House Hotel where they were created by the chef over a century ago and are still served, these white dinner rolls are brushed with butter before being folded into their characteristic shape. An early recipe for making the rolls appears in Fannie Farmer's 1898 Boston Cooking School Cook Book so perhaps she became an early fan after sampling them at the hotel.

MAKES: 24 rolls

BAKING TIME: 15–20 minutes

1½ cups milk

½ cup (4 oz) shortening, cut up

3 Tbsp superfine sugar

2 tsp salt

5–5¾ cups (1½–1¾ lb) bread flour, plus extra for kneading

1 Tbsp quick-rise yeast

½ cup warm water

2 large eggs, beaten

oil, for greasing

about ½ cup (4 oz) butter, softened until easy to spread

1 Heat the milk in a saucepan until it comes to the boil. Remove from the heat and stir in the shortening, sugar and salt. Set aside to cool until the milk is lukewarm.

2 Sift 2½ cups (12 oz) flour into a bowl and stir in the yeast. Add the cooled milk mixture, the water and eggs and stir until combined. Work in the enough of the remaining flour with your hands to make a soft but not sticky dough.

3 Knead with your hands for 10 minutes on a floured surface or in an electric mixer fitted with a dough hook for 5 minutes until smooth and elastic. Place the dough in an oiled bowl, cover with plastic wrap and leave to rise in a warm place until doubled in size.

4 Punch the dough down and knead again for 1–2 minutes. Roll it out to ½ inch thickness and stamp out 24 disks with a floured 3-inch plain cookie cutter, gathering up and re-rolling the trimmings as necessary.

5 Spread each disk on one side with a little softened butter and score the centers with the back of a knife, just slightly off center. Fold the smaller side over the larger and press the dough edges together to seal.

6 Place on greased baking sheets about 1 inch apart, cover loosely with greased plastic wrap and leave to rise until almost doubled in size.

7 Preheat the oven to 350°F and bake for 15–20 minutes or until the rolls are nicely browned.

TIP For a classic bagel filling, split them in half and spread the bottom halves with cream cheese. Top with slices of smoked salmon, sliced red onion, capers and sliced pickles. Add a squeeze of lemon juice and a few grindings of black pepper, replace the lids and serve.

bagels

Originally from Poland, these Jewish rolls were traditionally baked as an alternative to bublik, a special wheat bread eaten during Lent. Polish-Jewish immigrants took them first to London's East End and then to North America, where they are particularly popular in New York City. Unlike most breads, bagels are boiled briefly before they are baked, which gives them their unique spongy texture and chewy crust.

MAKES: 12 bagels

BAKING TIME: 20–25 minutes

1½ cups (7 oz) strong bread flour, plus extra for dusting

1 Tbsp superfine sugar

1 tsp quick-rise dried yeast

½ tsp salt

½ cup warm milk

2 Tbsp butter, melted

1 egg, separated

oil, for greasing

2 Tbsp sesame seeds, onion seeds, wheat germ or poppy seeds, for sprinkling

1 Sift the flour into a mixing bowl and stir in the sugar, yeast and salt. Make a well in the center and pour in the milk and melted butter. Add the egg white and mix to make a dough.

2 Turn the dough out onto a floured surface and knead for about 10 minutes by hand or for 5 minutes in an electric stand mixer fitted with a dough hook or until the dough is smooth and elastic.

3 Place the dough in an oiled bowl, cover with plastic wrap and leave in a warm place for about 1 hour or until doubled in size.

4 Divide the dough into 12 even-size pieces and shape into balls. Form into rings by pushing a floured finger into the center of each dough ball. Work your finger right the way through and rotate it until the hole becomes wider. To enlarge the hole, spin the dough ring around your finger to stretch it evenly until the hole is about one-third of the diameter of the whole bagel.

5 Place the bagels well apart on a floured baking sheet, cover with a dry kitchen towel and leave to rise for 15 minutes.

6 Preheat the oven to 400°F. Bring a large saucepan of water to the boil and add 2 or 3 dough rings. Poach them for 30 seconds before lifting them out with a large slotted spoon to allow excess water to drain off. Place on a greased baking sheet. Poach all the bagels in the same way, draining them well and placing on the baking sheet.

7 Mix the egg yolk with 1 tsp water and it brush over the tops of the bagels. Sprinkle over seeds of your choice or wheat germ and bake for 20–25 minutes until golden. Cool on a wire rack.

hot dog buns

In 1870, a German immigrant called Charles Feltman introduced hot dogs to the crowds of New Yorkers who were escaping the heat of summer in the city for the cooling breezes of Coney Island. Today the place to buy your hot dogs is Nathan's, which has become as much a part of the Coney Island experience as strolling along the famous boardwalk or braving the ups and downs of the Cyclone.

MAKES: 8 buns

BAKING TIME: 10 minutes

FOR THE BUNS

4 cups (1 lb 2 oz) strong white plain flour, plus extra if kneading by hand

1 tsp salt

1 Tbsp quick-rise yeast

¼ cup (2 oz) unsalted butter, diced

1 cup lukewarm milk

2 large eggs, beaten

1 Tbsp superfine sugar

oil for greasing

TO SERVE

Fried onions, hot dogs, mustard, relishes, dill pickles

1 To make the dough, sift the flour and salt into a mixing bowl and stir in the yeast. Rub in the butter until mixture resembles fine breadcrumbs then stir in the milk, eggs and sugar, and mix to a dough.

2 Turn out the dough onto a lightly floured surface and knead for about 10 minutes by hand or for 5 minutes in an electric mixer fitted with a dough hook. The dough needs to be smooth and elastic so work in a little more flour if it is very sticky.

3 Place the dough in an oiled bowl, cover with plastic wrap and leave to rise in a warm place for 1½–2 hours or until doubled in size.

4 Knock the dough down and divide it into 8 even-size pieces. Roll each piece into a ball and then shape into fingers about 6 inches long. Place the dough fingers on a greased baking sheet, leaving space between them so they have room to rise.

5 Cover the baking sheet with a damp kitchen towel and leave in a warm place for 30–40 minutes or until the dough fingers have doubled in size and are just touching each other.

6 Preheat the oven to 425°F and bake for 10 minutes or until golden on top. Pull the buns apart and transfer to a wire rack to cool.

7 Cut the buns in half down the center and open them up. Fill with fried onions and hot dogs and serve with mustard, relishes and dill pickles.

walnut bread

Baked in a muffin pan, these mini walnut loaves are delicious served warm for breakfast spread with butter or for a quick lunch or supper with cheese, cherry tomatoes, cucumber and pickles.

MAKES: 12 mini loaves

BAKING TIME: 30–35 minutes

3 cups (14 oz) bread flour, plus extra for kneading

¾ cup (3 oz) rye flour

1 Tbsp quick-rise dried yeast

2 tsp salt

½ cup warm water

½ cup warm milk

2 Tbsp liquid honey

1 Tbsp walnut oil, plus extra for greasing

½ cup chopped walnuts

1 Sift the bread flour into the bowl of an electric stand mixer with a dough hook fitted and stir in the rye flour, yeast and salt.

2 Mix together the water, milk, honey and walnut oil and pour into the dry ingredients. Add the walnuts and, with the mixer on low speed, knead for 5 minutes to make a smooth, elastic dough.

3 Transfer the dough to a greased bowl, cover with plastic wrap and leave in a warm place for around 2 hours or until doubled in size.

4 Knock the dough down with your fist. Dust the work surface with flour and knead the dough on it by hand for 1–2 minutes. Shape it into a rectangle and cut into 12 even-size pieces with a floured knife.

5 Grease a 12-cup muffin pan, roll the dough pieces into balls and put one in each muffin cup. Cover the pan with a damp kitchen towel and leave in a warm place to rise for about 1 hour or until doubled in size.

6 Preheat the oven to 450°F and bake the loaves for 5 minutes then reduce the temperature to 400°F and bake for a further 25–30 minutes or until the loaves sound hollow when tapped on the base.

7 Remove the loaves from the pan and transfer to a wire rack. Cover with a dry kitchen towel and leave until cool enough to handle before serving.

picnic knots

Don't keep these little rolls just for a picnic as they're good to eat at any time. Serve them with butter and marmalade for breakfast, as an accompaniment to a hearty lunchtime soup or with cheese and pickles for a late supper.

MAKES: 10 knots

BAKING TIME 20 minutes

2½ cups (12 oz) bread flour, plus extra if kneading by hand

4 tsp superfine sugar

1½ tsp quick-rise yeast

½ tsp salt

⅔ cup warm milk

3 Tbsp butter, melted and cooled

1 egg, beaten

oil, for greasing

1 egg yolk beaten with 2 Tbsp cold water, to glaze

⅓ cup sesame seeds

1 Sift the flour into a mixing bowl and stir in the sugar, yeast and salt. Make a well in the center of the dry ingredients and pour in the milk, butter and egg. Mix to make a soft dough.

2 Turn the dough out onto a lightly floured surface and knead by hand for 10 minutes or in an electric mixer fitted with a dough hook for 5 minutes, until smooth and elastic. Place the dough in an oiled bowl, cover with plastic wrap and leave to rise in a cool place for 1½–2 hours or until doubled in size.

3 Punch the dough down and knead it again for another 1–2 minutes. Cut into 10 even-size pieces, keeping the dough you are not working with covered with a sheet of oiled plastic wrap.

4 Roll out each piece of dough to a sausage about 8 inches long and carefully tie into knots. Divide the dough knots between two greased baking sheets, cover with oiled plastic wrap and leave to rise for about 30 minutes or until doubled in size.

5 Preheat the oven to 400°F. Brush the knots with the beaten egg yolk and sprinkle over the sesame seeds. Bake for about 20 minutes or until golden brown and a roll sounds hollow when tapped on the base. Slide onto a wire rack to cool.

cardamom crusts

Whether you have them spread with butter for breakfast or on their own with your morning coffee, these aromatic rolls, split through the middle and dried out in the oven until crunchy and light, make an unusual alternative to a slice of plain bread or toast. You could also cut them into smaller pieces to serve with dips.

MAKES: 60–70 crusts

BAKING TIME: 10 minutes
(plus drying time for crusts)

3 cups (13 oz) all-purpose flour, plus extra or sprinkling and kneading

⅓ cup (2 oz) granulated sugar

1 Tbsp quick-rise dried yeast

½ tsp salt

1 cup warm milk

½ cup (4 oz) butter, melted, plus 2 Tbsp melted butter

2 tsp cardamom seeds, crushed

2 Tbsp canola oil

1 Sift the flour into a mixing bowl and stir in the sugar, yeast and salt.

2 Mix together the warm milk and ½ cup of melted butter, make a well in the center of the dry ingredients and pour in the milk and butter. Add the crushed cardamom seeds and work everything together to make a smooth dough that comes away from the sides of the bowl, adding a little more flour if necessary.

3 Dust the dough with flour, cover with plastic wrap and leave it to rise in a warm place for 45 minutes.

4 Transfer the dough to a floured surface and knead for 5 minutes. Divide it into 4 even-size pieces and roll out each piece to a rectangle. Cut each into 16 pieces.

5 Put the pieces on baking sheets lined with parchment paper, cover with a damp kitchen towel and leave to rise in a warm place for 30 minutes.

6 Preheat the oven to 475°F. Mix 2 Tbsp melted butter with the canola oil and brush over the pieces of dough. Bake in the middle of the oven for 10 minutes.

7 Remove the crusts from the oven and leave them to cool. Cut each one in half through the middle and return the halves to the baking sheets. Reduce the oven temperature to 250°F and dry the crusts out in the oven until they are light and brittle.

apple bread

Dried apple pieces and apple juice make these much more interesting than plain rolls. Made using both a starter dough and main dough, the starter is mixed cold and left overnight, which gives the finished bread added flavor. Manitoba cream flour is used to make both doughs and it gives the loaf a lighter, fluffier texture.

MAKES: 16 rolls

BAKING TIME: 10–15 minutes

FOR THE STARTER DOUGH

5½ cups (1 lb 10 oz) Manitoba cream flour

½ tsp quick-rise dried yeast

2 cups cold water

FOR THE MAIN DOUGH

5¾ cups (1 lb 12 oz) Manitoba cream flour, plus extra for kneading

1 Tbsp quick-rise dried yeast

One-quarter of a batch of starter dough (made the day before)

2 cups warm apple juice

2 tsp table salt

¾ cup dried apple pieces, chopped

oil, for greasing

coarse sea salt, for sprinkling

1 To make the starter dough, sift the flour into a bowl and mix in the yeast. Add the water and mix to a dough. Transfer to a plastic container, cover with a lid and leave overnight.

2 To make the main dough, sift the flour into the bowl of an electric stand mixer fitted with a dough hook and stir in the yeast. Add the starter dough, apple juice and 2 tsp salt and knead on low speed for 5 minutes. Add the apples pieces, knead again until mixed in then cover the bowl with a damp kitchen towel and leave the dough to rise in a warm place for 45–60 minutes or until doubled in size.

3 Transfer the dough to a floured surface and knead by hand for 1–2 minutes. Divide it into 16 even-size pieces and shape them into small rolls. Place on greased baking sheets, cover with damp kitchen towels and leave to rise in a warm place for about 45 minutes or until doubled in size.

4 Preheat the oven to 450°F. Spray the rolls with water and sprinkle coarse sea salt over them. Bake for 10–15 minutes or until golden. Transfer to a wire rack to cool.

sweet pepper and mushroom rolls

These colorful little buns combine red and yellow peppers with mushrooms and aromatic rosemary and they are ideal for splitting and filling with crumbled goat cheese or blue cheese, sprigs of peppery arugula and sliced tomatoes. Alternatively, enjoy them on their own with a wedge of Cheddar or another hard cheese and a spoonful of chutney or bread and butter pickles.

MAKES: 12 rolls

BAKING TIME: 30–35 minutes

2 Tbsp olive oil, plus extra for greasing

½ red bell pepper, deseeded and finely chopped

½ yellow bell pepper, deseeded and finely chopped

2oz mushrooms, finely chopped

2 tsp finely chopped fresh rosemary leaves

2½ cups (12 oz) bread flour, plus extra if kneading by hand

2 tsp quick-rise yeast

1 tsp salt

1 cup warm water

2 Tbsp butter, melted

milk, to glaze

1 Heat the olive oil in a skillet and cook the red and yellow bell peppers over a low heat until softened but not browned. Stir in the mushrooms and rosemary, cook for a further 1–2 minutes then drain on a plate lined with paper towel and leave to cool.

2 Sift the flour into a mixing bowl and stir in the yeast and salt. Add the warm water and melted butter and mix to a fairly sticky dough. Knead by hand on a floured surface for 10 minutes or in an electric mixer fitted with a dough hook for 5 minutes until the dough is smooth and elastic, working in a little more flour if needed.

3 Place the dough in a large oiled bowl, cover with plastic wrap and leave to rise in a warm place for about 1½ hours or until doubled in size.

4 Knock back the dough with your fist, transfer it to a floured surface or return it to the bowl of the electric mixer and knead again for 2–3 minutes, working the cooked bell peppers, mushrooms and rosemary into the dough so they are evenly distributed.

5 Divide the dough into 12 even-size balls and divide between 2 greased and parchment-paper-lined baking sheets. Cover with oiled plastic wrap and leave to rise in a warm place for about 30 minutes or until doubled in size.

6 Preheat the oven to 425°F. Remove the plastic wrap and brush the tops of the buns with a little milk. Bake for 20–25 minutes or until golden and well risen. Transfer the buns to a wire rack to cool completely or eat them warm from the oven.

traditional loaves

A mix of everyday breads including white milk loaf, sour dough, Boston brown bread and a multi-seeded sandwich loaf, plus international standbys like anchor bread from Sweden, French baguettes and rye bread from Russia, that are guaranteed to keep the family smiling.

white milk loaf

This simple loaf would be delicious spread with butter and homemade jam for an afternoon tea. Serve it warm from the oven so you can enjoy its freshly baked aroma as well.

MAKES: 1 loaf

BAKING TIME: 30–35 minutes

4⅓ cups (1 lb 5 oz) bread flour, plus extra for dusting

2 Tbsp granulated sugar

2 tsp salt

1½ tsp quick-rise yeast

scant 1 cup warm milk

1½ Tbsp butter, melted and cooled

oil and a little extra melted butter, for greasing

1 Sift the flour into a large mixing bowl and stir in the sugar, salt and yeast.

2 Add the warm milk and melted butter and mix to a dough that should be soft but feel a little sticky when you squeeze it with your hands. If the dough clings to your fingers, add a little more flour.

3 Transfer the dough to a lightly floured surface and knead by hand for 5 minutes or knead in an electric mixer fitted with a dough hook for 3 minutes.

4 Put the dough in a clean, oiled bowl, cover with plastic wrap and leave in a warm place for about 1½ hours to rise until doubled in size.

5 Grease a 9- x 5-inch loaf pan by brushing with melted butter and dust with flour. Punch the risen dough down with your hand, knead again for a couple of minutes and then shape into a loaf.

6 Place the dough in the pan and cover with a clean kitchen towel. Leave to rise in a warm place for about 1 hour or until the dough has puffed up in the pan.

7 Preheat the oven to 375°F. Place the pan on a baking sheet and bake for 30–35 minutes or until the crust is a deep golden brown and the loaf sounds hollow when tapped. Leave to cool in the pan for 5 minutes before turning the loaf out onto a wire rack. Allow to rest for 20 minutes before slicing and serving warm or leave to cool completely.

whole wheat bread

Here's a really easy, straightforward loaf that has a slightly sweet taste. You'll find dozens of ways to use it and, as it can be frozen, you can make a couple of extras for later.

MAKES: 1 loaf

BAKING TIME: 30–35 minutes

4½ cups (1 lb 2 oz) strong whole wheat bread flour

2 tsp quick-rise dried yeast

1 tsp salt

1⅓ cups warm water

2 Tbsp olive oil
1 Tbsp liquid honey

1 Put the flour, yeast and salt into a mixing bowl and stir until mixed. Then stir in the water, oil and honey and mix to a soft dough.

2 Turn the dough out onto a lightly floured surface and knead for 5 minutes, until the dough no longer feels sticky, sprinkling with a little more flour if needed.

3 Grease a 9- x 5-inch loaf pan and put the dough into it, pressing it in evenly. Cover with a damp kitchen towel or oiled plastic wrap and leave in a warm place to rise for about 1 hour, until the dough has risen to fill the pan and no longer springs back when you press it with your finger.

4 Toward the end of the rising time, preheat the oven to 400°F.

5 Bake for 30–35 minutes until the loaf is risen and golden. Cool in the pan for 5 minutes, then place on a wire rack to cool completely.

pioneer bread

Here's a really simple, fruity bread that is delightful with coffee. It doesn't freeze well – but it's so good, there probably won't be any leftover, anyway.

MAKES: 1 loaf

BAKING TIME: 1 hour

2 cups (9 oz) all-purpose flour

¾ cup (3½ oz) whole wheat flour

1 cup (8 oz) granulated sugar

½ tsp salt

¼ tsp baking soda

1 Tbsp baking powder

¾ cup (4½ oz) chopped nuts

**1 cup (5 oz) dried fruit
(raisins, currants or raisins)**

1 large egg

⅓ cup sunflower oil

1 cup milk

1 tsp vanilla

1 Preheat the oven to 350°F. Grease a 9- x 5-inch loaf pan.

2 In a large bowl, mix together all the dry ingredients, except the fruit and nuts, until they are well blended. Then stir in the fruit and nuts.

3 Whisk the egg with the oil, milk and vanilla and stir it into the flour mixture.

4 Put the mixture in the pan and spread it evenly. Bake for about 1 hour until a skewer inserted into the center of the loaf comes out clean. Cool in the pan for 5 minutes, then place on a rack to cool completely.

baguettes

In France, bakers use a special flour called type 55 to make the nation's favorite loaves. Soft and low in gluten, the flour doesn't absorb much water so baguettes don't keep well and quickly go hard. The loaves were traditionally baked using a sourdough method but with the advent of supermarket in-store bakeries this became impractical and now gluten powder is added to the flour.

MAKES: 2–3 baguettes

BAKING TIME: 15–20 minutes

1 batch of basic white bread dough (see recipe on page 20)

1 Make up the dough as directed and leave it in a warm place to rise for the first time.

2 Transfer the dough to a floured surface and divide it into 2 or 3 even-size pieces. Shape into long baguettes without kneading them too much. Twist the lengths of dough several times before putting them on a greased baking sheet.

3 Cover with a damp cloth and leave in a warm place to rise for about 30 minutes or until doubled in size.

4 Preheat the oven to its highest setting and put a roasting pan half-filled with water in the bottom.

5 Make several diagonal cuts in the top of each baguette using a floured sharp knife and spray them with water using a spray bottle. Bake for 15–20 minutes until golden brown. Serve warm or cold.

SERVING SUGGESTIONS

• Baguettes make excellent crostini and bruschetta to serve as party food. Cut a baguette into thin slices on the diagonal and toast on both sides. Lay the slices on a baking sheet and top with cheese, salami, chopped red bell peppers, sliced mushrooms, cherry tomatoes or other ingredients of your choice. Brush with olive oil and heat through in a 350°F oven for 10 minutes. Serve at once.

• To make garlic bread, cut a baguette into slices without cutting all the way through. Lift it onto a sheet of foil large enough to wrap round it and spread garlic and herb butter between the slices. Reshape the loaf and spread more of the butter over the top. Wrap the foil tightly around the loaf and bake in a 425°F oven for 20 minutes. Open the foil and return the loaf to the oven for 5 minutes. Serve as soon as the bread is cool enough to handle.

bara brith

Bara Brith means 'speckled bread' in Welsh and this traditional sweet tea bread was originally only made for special occasions. Today's bakers don't wait for a special celebration to come along but make the loaves all year round so they can be enjoyed at any time, sliced and spread generously with butter.

MAKES: 1 loaf

BAKING TIME: 45 minutes

3⅓ cups (1 lb) bread flour, plus extra if kneading by hand

1 tsp ground mixed spice

½ tsp salt

¼ cup (2 oz) butter, at room temperature

1½ cups mixed dried fruit, including chopped candied peel

¼ cup (2 oz) light brown sugar

1½ tsp quick-rise yeast

1 cup warm milk

1 large egg, beaten

oil, for greasing

1 Sift the flour, mixed spice and salt in a mixing bowl and rub in the butter. Stir in the dried fruit, brown sugar and yeast.

2 Add the milk and most of the beaten egg, reserving a little for glazing the top of the loaf. Mix to a dough, adding a little extra flour if it is very wet or a little more milk if it seems too dry.

3 Turn out the dough and knead on a floured surface for 10 minutes or in an electric mixer fitted with a dough hook for 5 minutes until smooth and elastic. Transfer to an oiled bowl, cover with oiled plastic wrap and leave in a warm place for about 2 hours or until doubled in size.

4 Knead the dough again for 1–2 minutes then shape it into a rectangle and place in a greased 9- x 5-inch loaf pan. Cover loosely with greased plastic wrap and leave to rise again in a warm place until the dough reaches the top of the pan.

5 Preheat the oven to 400°F. Remove the plastic wrap and brush the top of the loaf with the reserved egg. Bake for 45 minutes, covering the top of the loaf with a sheet of foil after 25 minutes to stop it over-browning.

6 Cool the loaf in the pan for 10 minutes before turning it out onto a wire rack to cool completely. Eat fresh, sliced and buttered.

italian country bread

Although this deliciously crusty loaf needs a starter dough, the recipe can be completed in one day. Adding egg white to the dough makes it much more elastic, and brushing it with water before baking creates a wonderful crust.

MAKES: 1–2 loaves

BAKING TIME: 30 minutes

FOR THE STARTER DOUGH

3½ cups (1 lb) strong white bread flour

1¼ cups (8 oz) semolina flour

1 Tbsp quick-rise dried yeast

5½ cups warm water

FOR THE MAIN DOUGH

1 ⅔ cups (8 oz) strong white bread flour

½ cup plus 2 Tbsp olive oil

1 egg white

4 tsp salt

1 To make the starter dough, sift the bread flour into a bowl of an electric stand mixer and stir in the semolina flour and dried yeast. Pour in the water and mix in until combined. Cover the bowl with plastic wrap and set the dough aside in a warm place to rise for 60 minutes.

2 When the starter dough has risen, make the main dough. Add the bread flour, olive oil, egg white and salt to the starter dough and mix for 5 minutes on low speed to make a smooth, elastic dough.

3 Transfer the dough to a floured surface and shape into 1 large or 2 smaller loaves.

4 Lift the dough onto a greased baking sheet, cover with a damp kitchen towel and leave to rise in a warm place for about 40 minutes or until doubled in size. Cut slits in the top of the dough with a floured sharp knife.

5 Preheat the oven to 450°F, brush the dough with water and bake for 30 minutes until golden brown and crusty. Transfer to a wire rack to cool.

SERVING SUGGESTION

For a perfect lunch, fry a slice of Italian country bread and cover it with a sliced hard-cooked egg, mayonnaise and shelled cooked shrimp and garnish with dill.

boston brown bread

When we think of bread we think of baking but this wholesome, traditional loaf from New England is very much the exception, as it is steamed in food cans slowly in a pan on top of the stove. Considered by many Bostonians to be the only correct accompaniment to their famous baked beans, the bread can also be served for breakfast with bacon, drizzled with maple syrup.

MAKES: 2 loaves

BAKING TIME: about 3 hours

oil, for greasing

1 cup (4 oz) whole wheat bread flour

1 cup (4 oz) rye flour

¾ cup (4 oz) fine cornmeal

2 tsp baking soda

1 tsp salt

2 cups buttermilk

¾ cup molasses

¾ cup chopped pitted dates

1 Wash and dry two empty 1 lb food cans and brush the insides with oil.

2 In a mixing bowl, mix together the whole wheat flour, rye flour, cornmeal, baking soda and salt.

3 Pour in the buttermilk and molasses, add the chopped dates and stir everything together until evenly combined. Divide the mixture between the two cans, filling them about two-thirds full. Cover the cans tightly with a double layer of foil.

4 Place the cans on a rack in a deep saucepan, casserole or steamer and pour in enough boiling water to come up to the level of the rack. Cover the pan, bring the water back to the boil and adjust the heat so the water keeps boiling gently, topping it up as necessary during cooking.

5 Steam the bread for about 3 hours or until a skewer pushed into the center of each loaf comes out clean. Carefully lift out the cans, loosen the sides of the loaves by running a knife around them and turn them out immediately.

6 Serve the bread warm, cutting into slices with a serrated knife.

"anchor" loaf

This classic Swedish bread dates from the 1700s. Made for the military by the bakers to the royal household, it was a high-status bread that could be enjoyed only by officers. Its name derives from the shape of the wood used to make a ship's anchor that the loaf is said to resemble.

MAKES: 4–8 loaves

BAKING TIME: 30–40 minutes

FOR THE STARTER DOUGH

1¼ cups (4½ oz) rye flour, sifted

2 Tbsp quick-rise dried yeast

1¼ cups cold water

FOR THE MAIN DOUGH

2¾ cups warm water

¼ cup (2 oz) butter, melted

1¼ cups (9 oz) brown sugar

4 tsp salt

1 Tbsp soy sauce

7 cups (1 lb 9 oz) rye flour, sifted, plus extra for dusting

3 cups (14 oz) strong white bread flour

oil and milk, for glazing

1 To make the starter dough, put the rye flour into a bowl and stir in the yeast. Add the water and mix thoroughly. Cover the bowl with plastic wrap and leave it in the fridge overnight.

2 To make the main dough, transfer the starter dough to the bowl of an electric stand mixer fitted with a dough hook. Mix the warm water and melted butter together and add to the mixer bowl with the sugar, salt and soy sauce and mix well.

3 Add the rye flour and bread flour and knead the dough in the mixer on low speed for 8–10 minutes. Cover the bowl with a damp kitchen towel and leave the dough to rise in a warm place for about 30 minutes.

4 Transfer the dough to a surface dusted with rye flour and divide it into 4 or 8 pieces. Shape each piece into a loaf and place them on a baking sheet lined with parchment paper. Brush the tops and sides of the loaves with oil, cover with plastic wrap and leave to rise again for 30 minutes.

5 Preheat the oven to 400°F. Bake the loaves on the bottom shelf of the oven for 30–40 minutes or until they sound hollow when tapped underneath.

6 Remove the loaves from the oven and brush the tops with a little milk. Cover with a dry kitchen towel and leave to cool on the baking sheet.

potato loaf

This bread is made with the same starter dough of Manitoba cream flour as apple bread (see page 50). Although there is not much yeast in the dough, the quality of the flour makes a light and fluffy loaf. Spraying water into the hot oven before you bake the loaf creates steam and gives the bread a crisper crust.

MAKES: 1–2 loaves

BAKING TIME: 15–20 minutes

3 large boiled potatoes

Half a batch of Manitoba starter dough (see recipe on page 60)

2 cups (9 oz) all-purpose flour, plus extra for kneading and dusting

¼ cup corn oil, plus extra for greasing

1 Mash the boiled potatoes until they are smooth.

2 Mix the starter dough into the potatoes with the all-purpose flour and oil. Knead by hand on a floured surface for 10 minutes or in an electric stand mixer with a dough hook for 5 minutes. Cover the dough with a damp kitchen towel and leave it to rise for 30 minutes or until doubled in size.

3 Knock the dough down and turn it out onto a floured surface. Knead it by hand for 1–2 minutes then shape the dough into one large or two smaller loaves. Place in floured rising baskets or wrap in clean, floured kitchen towels and leave to rise under a cloth for 1 hour or until the dough has doubled in size.

4 Put the bread on a greased baking sheet. Preheat the oven to 450°F and spray water over the bottom of the oven. Reduce the oven temperature to 400°F and bake for 15–20 minutes or until the bread sounds hollow when tapped on the base.

5 Transfer the bread to a wire rack, cover with a dry kitchen towel and let cool.

EXPERT ADVICE

Some doughs for large loaves often need to be supported during the second rise. This can be done either by putting the shaped dough in a rising basket or by wrapping it in a floured kitchen towel. If the bread is in a basket, turn it out carefully onto a greased baking sheet when it is ready for baking so you don't deflate it.

TIP The dough can also be made into saffron buns. Divide it into 12 even-size pieces and, dusting your hands with flour, roll each piece into a ball. Place on a greased baking sheet, leaving space between them to rise, cover with a damp kitchen towel and leave to rise until doubled in size. Bake the buns for 15 minutes at 400°F, lower the temperature to 350°F and bake for a further 5 minutes. Glaze with the melted butter and sugar and return to the oven for 3 minutes.

fruited cornish saffron loaf

In Medieval times saffron was grown in Cornwall, in the far southwest of the British Isles, and bakers began adding the delicate threads to their doughs to give them a warm, golden glow. Saffron loaves and buns are still popular in Cornwall today with the locally produced clotted cream a favorite accompaniment.

MAKES: 1 loaf

BAKING TIME: about 50 minutes

1 tsp saffron strands

2 Tbsp hot water

3½ cups (1 lb) strong plain white flour, plus extra for kneading

½ tsp salt

1 Tbsp quick-rise yeast

⅔ cup (5 oz) unsalted butter, diced

1⅓ cups raisins

⅓ cup chopped mixed peel

¼ cup (2 oz) superfine sugar

1 tsp ground cinnamon

½ tsp ground allspice

¼ tsp grated nutmeg

½ cup warm milk

2 large eggs

oil, for greasing

TO GLAZE

2 Tbsp unsalted butter, melted

2 Tbsp superfine sugar

1 Crumble the saffron strands between your fingers into a small heatproof bowl. Add the hot water and set aside to soak for 30 minutes.

2 Sift the flour and salt into a mixing bowl and stir in the yeast. Rub in the butter until the mixture resembles fine breadcrumbs. Stir in the raisins, mixed peel, sugar, cinnamon, allspice and nutmeg.

3 Beat together the warm milk and eggs and add to the dry ingredients with the saffron and its soaking water. Stir to mix then work everything together to make a soft dough. Transfer the dough to a lightly floured surface and knead for about 10 minutes by hand or in an electric mixer fitted with a dough hook for 5 minutes until it is smooth and elastic.

4 Transfer the dough to an oiled bowl, cover with plastic wrap and leave in a warm place for 3–4 hours or until doubled in size.

5 Grease a 9- x 5-inch loaf pan. Knock the dough down, transfer to a floured surface and knead for 1–2 minutes. Shape it into a loaf and place in the pan, seam side down. Cover with a damp kitchen towel and leave to rise again in a warm place for about 2 hours or until the dough rises to the top of the pan.

6 Preheat the oven to 400°F, place the pan on a baking sheet and bake for 20 minutes. Lower the oven temperature to 350°F and bake for a further 25–30 minutes or until the base of the loaf sounds hollow when tapped. Glaze the top of the loaf by brushing with the melted butter and sprinkling over the sugar. Return to the oven for a further 3 minutes before turning the loaf out onto a wire rack to cool. Serve cut into slices, spread with butter or thick cream and jam.

multi-seed sandwich loaf

An excellent loaf for everyday eating as not only does it make very good sandwiches, it's great for toast too. You can use any mix of seeds you wish or replace one of the seeds with chopped nuts or rolled oats.

MAKES: 1 loaf

BAKING TIME: 45 minutes

3¾ cups (1 lb) plain whole wheat bread flour, plus extra if kneading by hand

2 tsp quick-rise yeast

1½ tsp salt

1½ cups warm water

½ cup sunflower seeds

3 Tbsp sesame seeds

3 Tbsp poppy seeds

3 Tbsp pumpkin seeds

2 Tbsp sunflower oil, plus extra for greasing

2 tsp dark muscovado sugar

1 Mix the flour, yeast and salt together in a large mixing bowl. Pour in the water, then add all the seeds, oil and sugar and mix to make a dough.

2 Turn out the dough onto a lightly floured surface and knead for 10 minutes by hand or for 5 minutes in an electric mixer fitted with a dough hook. Transfer the dough to an oiled bowl, cover with plastic wrap and leave to rise for 1½ hours in a warm place or until doubled in size.

3 Push the dough down with your fist and knead again for a few minutes on a lightly floured surface. Shape into a rectangle and place in a greased 9- x 5-inch loaf pan.

4 Cover with oiled plastic wrap and leave to rise until the dough has doubled in size – this will take about 45 minutes.

5 Preheat the oven to 400°F. Set the pan on a baking sheet and bake for 40 minutes or until the base of the loaf sounds hollow when tapped. Place the turned-out loaf on the baking sheet and return it to the oven for 5 minutes so the edges crisp a little.

rye bread

Rye bread is particularly popular in Scandinavia but when made with just rye flour the loaves are pretty dense and heavy so you may prefer this version that uses a mixture of white bread flour and rye flour. The combination makes a lighter loaf but you can of course vary the proportions of the flours according to personal taste. If you increase the quantity of rye flour to make a darker loaf you may need to increase the quantity of water added to the dough.

MAKES: I loaf

BAKING TIME: 40 minutes

¾ cup warm milk

¾ cup warm water

2 Tbsp dark brown soft sugar

1½ cups (7 oz) bread flour, plus extra for dusting

2½ cups (9 oz) rye flour

I Tbsp salt

1½ tsp quick-rise dried yeast

I tsp caraway seeds

I tsp fennel seeds

oil, for greasing

1 Stir the milk, water and sugar together. Sift the white flour into a large bowl and stir in the rye flour, salt, yeast, caraway seeds and fennel seeds.

2 Make a well in the center of the dry ingredients and pour in the milk mixture. Mix with a wooden spoon and then your hands to bring everything together to make a soft dough.

3 Turn out the dough onto a surface dusted with flour and knead by hand for 10 minutes or in an electric stand mixer fitted with a dough hook for 5 minutes or until the dough is smooth and elastic.

4 Transfer the dough to an oiled bowl, cover with plastic wrap and leave to rise in a warm place for 1½–2 hours or until it has doubled in size.

5 Knock the dough down with your fist, turn it out onto a floured surface and knead by hand for 1–2 minutes. Shape the dough into a ball, lift it onto a baking sheet lined with parchment paper and score the top several times with a floured sharp knife.

6 Cover the dough loosely with oiled plastic wrap and leave it in a warm place to rise for about 45 minutes or until it has doubled in size.

7 Preheat the oven to 350ºF and bake the bread for 40 minutes or until the loaf sounds hollow when tapped on the base. Serve warm or cold.

russian rye bread

This bread is made with a starter dough of rye flour and sour milk which is left to stand and rise overnight. Buy the best-quality rye flour that you can find as the end result will be well worth it.

MAKES: 3 loaves

BAKING TIME: 30–35 minutes

FOR THE STARTER DOUGH

2½ cups (9 oz) fine rye flour

2 tsp quick-rise dried yeast

2 cups cold sour milk (see Tip)

FOR THE MAIN DOUGH

2 cups warm water

2 Tbsp liquid honey

6½ cups (1 lb 8 oz) fine rye flour, plus extra for kneading

2 tsp quick-rise dried yeast

oil, for greasing

1 To make the starter dough, stir the rye flour and yeast together in a bowl. Add the sour milk and mix until it is combined with the dry ingredients. Cover the bowl with plastic wrap and leave the dough to rise in a cool place for 24 hours.

2 To make the main dough, mix the water and honey together and mix into the starter dough, stirring thoroughly. Stir together the rye flour and yeast and work this into the starter dough. Knead the dough by hand on a floured surface for 10 minutes or in an electric stand mixer with a dough hook for 5 minutes.

3 Transfer the dough to an oiled bowl, cover with plastic wrap and leave it in a warm place for about 2 hours or until doubled in size.

4 Cut the dough into 3 even-size pieces with a floured knife and roll out each piece to a thick disk. Sprinkle the disks with flour and put them in rising baskets. Cover with damp kitchen towels and leave them to rise in a warm place for about

40 minutes or until doubled in size. If you don't have rising baskets, wrap in clean, floured kitchen towels and leave to rise under a cloth for about 40 minutes or until the dough has doubled in size.

5 Preheat the oven to 425°F. Carefully transfer the loaves to baking sheets lined with parchment paper and cut a cross in the top of each one.

6 Spray water onto the bottom of the oven and bake the bread for 10 minutes. Reduce the oven temperature to 425°F and bake the loaves for a further 20–25 minutes or until they sound hollow when tapped on the base. Transfer the bread to wire racks to cool.

TIP You can make sour milk by adding 2 Tbsp white vinegar or lemon juice to a 2-cup measure, pouring in enough milk to yield 2 cups, then letting it stand for a couple of minutes.

levain or sourdough bread

This loaf has lots of flavor and as it is baked with Manitoba cream flour it will keep longer than ordinary bread.

MAKES: 2 loaves

BAKING TIME: 20–25 minutes

Three-quarters of a batch of plain sourdough starter (see recipe on page 33)

2¼ cups warm water

6 cups (1 lb 12 oz) Manitoba cream flour, plus extra for kneading

1 Tbsp salt

oil, for greasing

1 Put the sourdough starter in the bowl of an electric stand mixer with a dough hook and stir in the warm water. Mix in the flour and salt.

2 Mix on low speed for 5 minutes or transfer to a floured surface and knead by hand for 10 minutes or until the dough is smooth and elastic. Put the dough in an oiled bowl, cover with a damp kitchen towel and leave to rise at room temperature for 2½ hours until doubled in size. During the first hour, transfer the dough twice to a floured surface, knead it briefly and fold it over before returning it to the bowl.

4 Divide the risen dough in half, shape each half into a ball and place in rising baskets dusted with flour. Cover with damp kitchen towels and leave in a warm place for 1 hour to rise again. If you don't have rising baskets, wrap in clean, floured kitchen towels and leave to rise under a cloth for 1 hour or until the dough has doubled in size.

5 Preheat the oven to 450°F. Carefully transfer the loaves to baking sheets lined with parchment paper and cut a slash in the top of each one with a floured sharp knife.

6 Bake in the oven for 20–25 minutes or until the loaves sound hollow when tapped on the base.

english muffins

Very different from American muffins, recipes for these round, flat-topped English buns have been around since the mid-18th century. Celebrated in the children's nursery rhyme 'Do you know the Muffin-man…who lives in Drury Lane', the muffin man was a familiar sight on British streets before the First World War. He sold freshly made muffins from a tray that he balanced on his head on top of a padded cap and rang a hand-bell to announce his arrival to the local children.

MAKES: 8 muffins

COOKING TIME: about 40 minutes

3⅓ cups (1 lb) strong white bread flour

1½ tsp quick-rise yeast

1 tsp salt

¾ cup warm milk

⅔ cup warm water

2 Tbsp ground rice, for dusting

oil, for greasing

unsalted butter, for cooking

1 Sift the flour into a warm bowl – this will help give the muffins a lighter texture – and stir in the yeast and salt.

2 Make a well in the center and stir in the warm milk and water, stirring until mixed in. Dust your hands with ground rice and bring the mixture together with your hands then turn it out onto a surface dusted with more ground rice and knead for about 10 minutes until you have a soft, smooth dough that is no longer sticky. Alternately, knead the dough in an electric mixer fitted with a dough hook for 5–6 minutes.

3 Place the dough in an oiled bowl, cover with plastic wrap and leave to rise in a warm place for about 1 hour or until doubled in size.

4 Knock the dough down and divide it into eight even-size pieces. Dust your hands and the work surface or a board with ground rice and shape each piece of dough into a disk about ¾ inch thick. Flatten the tops of the muffins, sprinkle them with ground rice and cover loosely with plastic wrap. Leave in a warm place to rise for 30 minutes.

5 Heat a little butter on a griddle or in a heavy skillet and when the butter has melted and the griddle is moderately – but not very – hot, put four muffins around the edge of the griddle, which will be cooler than the center. Cook very gently for about 10 minutes on each side so the tops and bottoms of the muffins are browned and the insides just cooked.

6 Remove from the pan and cook the remaining four muffins in the same way. Split the warm muffins open, spread with butter and eat straight away. Or, allow them to cool, cut them open and toast on both sides. Fill the muffins with cold meats and salad.

TIP The muffins need to be cooked very slowly over a gentle heat or they will burn on the outside before they are done in the middle.

date bread

This loaf makes a wonderful Christmas treat but it's too good to keep just for the festive season; you'll want to make it all year round. To make the bread you need a rye sourdough starter and a pre-dough, which sounds like a lot of work but using both does give it a superb flavor.

MAKES: 2 loaves

BAKING TIME: 25–30 minutes

DAY 1

⅓ cup plus 2 Tbsp rye sourdough starter (see recipe on page 34)

1¼ cups (4½ oz) rye flour

1¼ cups warm water

DAY 2

4 cups (14 oz) sifted rye flour

1½ cups (7 oz) bread flour, plus extra for dusting

1¼ cups (8 oz) semolina flour

1 tsp quick-rise dried yeast

2 tsp salt

2¼ cups warm water

¾ cup pitted chopped dates

¼ cup molasses

1 On day 1 make the pre-dough by mixing the rye sourdough starter with the rye flour and warm water in a large bowl. Cover the bowl with plastic wrap and let the mixture stand at room temperature overnight.

2 On day 2 make the main dough. Mix the rye flour, bread flour, semolina flour and salt together in the bowl of an electric stand mixer fitted with a dough hook and stir in the yeast.

3 Add the warm water to the pre-dough until it is well combined then add this to the dry ingredients in the mixer bowl, along with the dates and molasses. Mix on low speed for 5 minutes until the dough is smooth and elastic then cover the bowl with plastic wrap and leave the dough in a warm place to rise until it doubles in size, 3–4 hours.

4 Turn out the dough onto a floured surface and, with floured hands, carefully flatten it out into a rectangle. Cut the dough in half and place the two halves on a baking sheet lined with parchment paper. Cover with a damp kitchen towel and leave to rise in a warm place for 1½ hours or until doubled in size.

5 Preheat the oven to its highest setting. Put a little water in a roasting pan and set this in the bottom of the oven. Bake the bread for 10 minutes then reduce the oven temperature to 400°F and bake for a further 15–20 minutes or until the loaves sound hollow when tapped on the base. Transfer to a wire rack to cool.

sour milk loaf with nuts and berries

As well as walnuts and blueberries, this tasty loaf also has sunflower seeds, flaxseeds and apricots added to the dough, which is made from a blend of all-purpose, whole wheat and brown spelt flours.

MAKES: 2 loaves

BAKING TIME: 1½ hours

4 cups sour milk

1 cup molasses

2 tsp baking soda

3 cups (13 oz) all-purpose flour

1⅔ cups (7 oz) whole wheat flour

¾ cup (3½ oz) brown spelt flour

1 cup sunflower seeds

1 cup flaxseeds

12 dried apricots, quartered

½ cup dried blueberries

½ cup coarsely chopped walnuts

2 tsp salt

1 Preheat the oven to 350°F.

2 Mix the sour milk with the molasses and baking soda and then stir in the other ingredients.

3 Divide the soft dough between 2 well-greased 9- by 5-inch loaf pans.

4 Bake the loaves in the oven for 1½ hours or until a metal skewer pushed into the center of each loaf comes out clean with no uncooked dough sticking to it.

5 Leave the loaves to cool in the pans for 5 minutes before turning them out. Cover them with a dry kitchen towel and leave until cool enough to handle before slicing.

cinnamon and raisin swirl

At first glance this looks like a simple iced fruit loaf but cut into it and you'll find an eye-catching spiral of cinnamon sugar running through the crumb. Although the loaf can be stored for a day or two in an airtight container, it is best eaten on the day it is made. If you wish the loaf can be drizzled or spread with a thin layer of white icing.

SERVES: 1 loaf

BAKING TIME: 30–35 minutes

3 cups (14 oz) bread flour, plus extra for kneading and shaping

5 Tbsp superfine sugar

1½ tsp quick-rise yeast

1 tsp salt

2 Tbsp unsalted butter, diced

4 Tbsp milk

about ¾ cup warm water

oil, for greasing

⅓ cup raisins

1½ Tbsp ground cinnamon

1 Sift the flour into a large mixing bowl and stir 3 Tbsp sugar, the yeast and the salt. Rub in the butter and then add the milk and enough of the water to make to a soft dough.

2 Turn out the dough onto a lightly floured surface and knead by hand for 10 minutes or in an electric mixer fitted with a dough hook for 5 minutes. Place the dough in a lightly oiled bowl, cover with plastic wrap and leave in a warm place to rise for about 1 hour or until the dough has doubled in size.

3 Transfer the dough to a lightly floured surface, sprinkle with the raisins and knead them into the dough. Roll or press it out to a rectangle measuring about 15 × 8 inches.

4 Mix together the cinnamon and the remaining sugar and sprinkle evenly over the dough. Dampen the edges and, starting at once short side, roll the dough up in a tight spiral like a jelly roll. Put seam side down in an oiled 9- × 5-inch loaf pan, cover loosely with oiled plastic wrap and leave in a warm place to prove until the dough has risen above the top of the pan.

5 Preheat the oven to 375°F. Place the pan on a baking sheet and bake the loaf until the top is golden brown. If the top becomes sufficiently brown before the loaf is ready cover it with a sheet of foil for the remainder of the cooking time.

6 Cool in the pan for 5 minutes before turning out onto a wire rack to cool completely.

nut bread

When walnuts are plentiful, this delicious crunchy bread is the best way to use them up. Better still, you can make extra loaves and freeze them to use later.

MAKES: 1 loaf

BAKING TIME: 35 minutes plus 10 minutes for the walnuts

1½ cups chopped walnuts

2½ cups (12 oz) bread flour

3 cups (12 oz) strong whole wheat bread flour

1 tsp salt

2 tsp quick-rise dried yeast

1⅔ cups warm water

2 Tbsp walnut oil

1 Tbsp liquid honey

1 Preheat the oven to 400°F and grease a baking sheet.

2 Put the walnuts on the baking sheet and toast them in the oven for 8–10 minutes until lightly browned. Set aside to cool.

3 Put both flours, along with the salt and the yeast in a mixing bowl and stir them to combine.

4 Mix together the water, walnut oil and honey and stir into the flour mixture, with the walnuts. Mix with your hands to a soft dough. If the dough is too stiff, add more warm water.

5 Turn the dough out onto a lightly floured surface and knead for 10 minutes. Shape the dough into a neat oval shape and place on the baking sheet. Cover with a kitchen towel and leave in a warm place to rise until doubled in size, about 1 hour

6 Bake for about 35 minutes until golden brown and sounds hollow when tapped on the base. Cool on a wire rack.

pumpkin-seed bread

The addition of pumpkin seeds to this loaf gives a delightful crunch and adds extra nutrition. Consider doubling the recipe and freezing one of the loaves for another time.

MAKES: 1 loaf

BAKING TIME: 25 minutes

2½ cups (12 oz) strong white bread flour

2 tsp quick-rise dried yeast

½ tsp salt

½ tsp light brown sugar

¾ cup warm water

2 Tbsp milk

1–2 Tbsp pumpkin seeds

1 Put the flour, yeast, salt and sugar into a mixing bowl and stir until well mixed.

2 Stir in the water and mix to a dough. Knead in the bowl for about 10 minutes, stretching and folding the dough until smooth and elastic. If the dough is too sticky, add more flour (or more water if too dry).

3 Put the mixture into a lightly oiled bowl, cover with oiled plastic wrap and leave in a warm place for about 1 hour, until doubled in size.

4 Turn out onto a lightly floured surface and knock back the dough.

5 Mold it into a round loaf shape and place it on a baking sheet lined with parchment paper. Cover with lightly oiled plastic wrap and leave in a warm place to rise for about 30 minutes, until doubled in size.

6 Toward the end of the rising time, preheat the oven to 450°F.

7 Brush the top of the loaf with the milk and sprinkle with the pumpkin seeds. Bake for about 25 minutes until it is golden and sounds hollow when tapped on the base. Place on a wire rack to cool.

festive breads

At Easter time in Russia Orthodox families bake a traditional kulich to be blessed by their local priest, Christmas in Italy is all about panettone, while in Germany mini stollen wrapped in cellophane and tied with a pretty ribbon make delightful presents. We celebrate festive seasons with special breads from around the world.

russian kulich

MAKES: I loaf

BAKING TIME: 35–40 minutes

FOR THE DOUGH

4⅓ cups (1 lb 5 oz) bread flour

I tsp ground cardamom

I tsp ground cinnamon

½ tsp salt

2 tsp quick-rise yeast

I¼ cups warm milk

½ cup (4 oz) very soft butter, cut into small pieces

⅓ cup (3 oz) superfine sugar

⅓ cup raisins

⅓ cup chopped candied citrus peel

3 eggs

oil, for greasing

FOR THE ICING AND DECORATION

I½ cups confectioners' sugar

about 2 Tbsp lemon juice

2 Tbsp toasted flaked almonds

2 Tbsp sugar sprinkles

In Russia kulich loaves are taken to church on Easter Saturday evening to be blessed by the priest before the feasting that follows on Easter Sunday when painted eggs are given as gifts. Kulich loaves are traditionally baked in tall cylindrical pans and, although recipes vary from family to family, the dough is usually flavored with sweet spices such as cardamom and cinnamon and with dried fruits and nuts often added. The tops of the baked loaves are frosted with white icing and sometimes a lighted candle is placed in the center.

1 To make the dough, sift the flour, cardamom, cinnamon and salt into the bowl of an electric mixer fitted with a dough hook and mix in the yeast.

2 Add the milk, butter, sugar, raisins, candied peel and eggs and mix for about 5 minutes on slow speed. Scrape out the dough onto a well-floured surface and shape into a ball. Place in a lightly oiled bowl, cover with oiled plastic wrap and leave to rise in a warm place for 1½–2 hours or until doubled in size.

3 Knock the dough down with your knuckles, shape it into a ball and place in a 7-inch kulich pan or panettone pan that has been greased and lined with parchment paper. Cover with oiled plastic wrap and leave until the dough rises almost to the top of the pan.

4 Preheat the oven to 350°F. Bake for 35–40 minutes or until golden brown and a skewer pushed into the center of the kulich comes out clean. Leave to cool in the pan before turning out onto a wire rack to cool completely.

5 To ice the kulich, sift the confectioners' sugar into a bowl and stir in enough lemon juice to make a thick, smooth icing. Spoon the icing over the loaf and decorate with the flaked almonds and sugar sprinkles scattered over. Leave until the icing has set. Cut into wedges to serve.

TIP The easiest way to make the dough is to use an electric mixer fitted with a dough hook as, although it can be made by hand, it is a messy operation as the dough is very sticky and must be kneaded for quite a long time to make it manageable.

greek christmas bread

MAKES: 1 loaf

BAKING TIME: 50 minutes

FOR THE DOUGH

2½–2¾ cups (12–13 oz) bread flour, plus extra if kneading by hand

3 Tbsp superfine sugar

finely grated zest of 1 orange

2 tsp quick-rise yeast

½ tsp salt

3 eggs

½ cup warm milk

⅓ cup liquid honey

⅓ cup (3 oz) unsalted butter, melted and cooled

1½ Tbsp light olive oil or sunflower oil, plus extra for greasing

4 dried figs, cut into small pieces

2 Tbsp chopped candied citrus peel

2 Tbsp golden raisins

1 Tbsp anise seeds

FOR THE GLAZE

1 small egg white

2 tsp superfine sugar

2 tsp liquid honey

4 walnut halves, broken into pieces

8 whole almonds

1 Tbsp chopped candied citrus peel

Known as Cristopsomo, meaning 'Christ's bread' in Greek, different versions of this loaf are baked in Orthodox homes during the festive season to ensure the health and well-being of the family during the coming year. Serve the bread plain or sliced and spread with butter.

1 To make the dough, sift 2½ cups (12 oz) flour into a large bowl and stir in the sugar, orange zest, yeast and salt. Beat together the eggs, milk, honey, melted butter and oil and add to the dry ingredients. Mix well then transfer to a floured surface and knead for 10 minutes, working in a little more flour if necessary to make a smooth, soft dough. Alternatively, knead the dough for 5–6 minutes in an electric mixer fitted with a dough hook until smooth and elastic.

2 Put the dough in a greased bowl, cover with plastic wrap and leave it in a warm place for about 1½ hours or until doubled in size.

3 Punch the dough down and knead again for 3–4 minutes by hand or in an electric mixer working in the figs, citrus peel, raisins and anise seeds. Shape the dough into a ball or a rectangular shape, or divide it into three and form into a braid. Place on a greased baking sheet and cover with oiled plastic wrap.

4 Leave in a warm place for about 30 minutes or until doubled in size.

5 Preheat the oven to 400°F. Bake for 10 minutes then reduce the oven temperature to 350°F.

6 To make the glaze, whisk the egg white until thick but not stiff and dry then whisk in the sugar and honey. Brush the top of the loaf generously with the glaze and gently push the walnut pieces into it. Sprinkle over the almonds and candied peel and brush again with the glaze. Bake for a further 40 minutes or until the loaf is golden brown. Transfer it to a wire rack to cool.

panettone

MAKES: 1 loaf

BAKING TIME: 55–60 minutes

3⅓ cups (1 lb) bread flour, plus extra if kneading by hand, and dusting

⅓ cup (3 oz) superfine sugar

Finely grated zest of 1 orange

Finely grated zest of 1 lemon

2½ tsp quick-rise yeast

1 tsp salt

4 egg yolks

1 egg

1 tsp vanilla extract

⅔ cup warm milk

¾ cup (6 oz) unsalted butter, diced and softened

¾ cup finely chopped candied citrus peel

½ cup raisins

oil, for greasing

1 lightly beaten egg white, to glaze (optional)

Brightly colored boxes containing panettone are a popular sight in Italian pasticceria windows, especially during the Christmas season. Originally from Milan but now eaten throughout Italy, panettone has a light, open-textured crumb that is half way between a bread and a cake. During the festive season, elaborate iced versions filled with chocolate, custard and candied fruits are produced, as well as the traditional plain loaves. In Italy, slices of panettone are usually accompanied with a tiny cup of fiercely strong espresso coffee or a glass of sweet dessert wine such as moscato, vin santo or Marsala.

1 Sift the flour into a mixing bowl and stir in the sugar, orange and lemon zest, yeast and salt. Beat together the egg yolks, egg and vanilla and pour into the dry ingredients with the milk.

2 Mix to make a soft dough and then knead by hand on a floured surface for 10 minutes or in an electric mixer fitted with a dough hook for 5 minutes or until smooth and elastic.

3 Gradually work in the butter and, when incorporated, shape the dough into a ball and place in a mixing bowl that has been dusted with flour rather than greased. Cover with plastic wrap and leave to rise for 2–3 hours or until doubled in size.

4 Knock down the risen dough and knead again for 1–2 minutes, working in the candied citrus peel and raisins. Shape the dough into a ball and place in a greased 7-inch panettone pan. Cut a cross in the top of the dough with a sharp knife, cover with oiled plastic wrap and leave to rise until tripled in size.

5 Preheat the oven to 400°F. Remove the plastic wrap and brush the top of the loaf with lightly beaten egg white or leave plain, as preferred. Bake for 15 minutes then lower the heat to 350°F and bake for a further 40–45 minutes or until risen and golden brown. Cool in the pan for 10 minutes before turning out on to a wire rack to cool completely.

TIP Sweet yeast doughs take longer than ordinary bread doughs to rise, but avoid the temptation to put the panettone in a very warm place as the butter in the dough will start to melt and make the dough fatty.

mini stollen

Wrapped in cellophane and tied with a pretty ribbon these miniature versions of the classic German Christmas bread would make lovely presents for special friends. The stollen can be baked ahead and frozen until needed.

MAKES: 6 mini stollen

BAKING TIME: 20–25 minutes

1 cup raisins

⅓ cup chopped almonds

¼ cup candied cherries, rinsed in warm water to remove their syrupy coating, dried and chopped

¼ cup chopped candied citrus peel

finely grated zest of 1 lemon

2 Tbsp brandy or orange juice

2½ cups (12 oz) bread flour, plus extra is kneading by hand

1 tsp ground cinnamon

½ tsp salt

¼ cup (2 oz) golden superfine sugar

2 tsp quick-rise yeast

about ⅔ cup warm milk

⅓ cup (3 oz) unsalted butter, melted

1 large egg, beaten

oil, for greasing

7 oz natural marzipan or almond paste

confectioners' sugar, to dust

1 Put the raisins, almonds, cherries, citrus peel and lemon zest in a bowl and stir in the brandy or orange juice. Set aside.

2 Sift the flour, cinnamon and salt into a mixing bowl and stir in the sugar and yeast. Add the milk, melted butter and beaten egg. Mix together to make a dough, adding a little more milk if the mixture is dry.

3 Transfer the dough to a lightly floured surface and knead for 10 minutes until smooth and elastic or knead it for 5 minutes in an electric mixer fitted with a dough hook. Place the dough in an oiled bowl and leave to rise in a warm place for about 1½ hours of until it has doubled in size.

4 Punch the dough down and turn it out onto a floured surface or return it to the bowl of the electric mixer. Gradually knead in the fruit mixture until it is evenly distributed throughout the dough. Cover with a damp kitchen towel and set the dough aside to rest for 20 minutes.

5 Divide the marzipan or almond paste into six equal pieces and roll each one into a log measuring about 4 inches. Knead the dough by hand for 1–2 minutes and divide it into six pieces. Roll each piece to a rectangle large enough to enclose a log of marzipan, place the marzipan just off center on each piece of dough and brush the edges lightly with water.

6 Fold the dough over the marzipan to enclose it completely, pressing the edges together to seal. Arrange on a lightly greased baking sheet, cover with oiled plastic wrap and leave in a warm place to rise until the stollen have doubled in size.

7 Preheat the oven to 350°F. Bake the stollen for 20–25 minutes or until risen and golden brown. Transfer to a wire rack to cool before dusting generously with confectioners' sugar.

st. lucia buns

On December 13 each year, Swedish bakers celebrate St Lucia Day by making these special saffron buns. The buns are baked in different shapes but the most popular shape is where the ends are curled inwards like a snail. Called 'lussekatt' in Swedish, the name translates as 'Lucia's cat' and as the buns resemble a curled up sleeping feline that is no doubt how they got their name.

MAKES: 12 buns

BAKING TIME: 15 minutes

1 tsp saffron threads

1 cup hot milk

3½ cups (1 lb 2 oz) bread flour, plus extra if kneading by hand

¼ cup (2 oz) superfine sugar

1½ tsp quick-rise yeast

1 tsp salt

¼ cup (2 oz) unsalted butter, melted

3½ oz curd cheese, such as ricotta

oil for greasing

1 egg yolk beaten with 1 Tbsp cold water, to glaze

24 raisins

1 Crumble the saffron into the hot milk and set aside until the milk cools and becomes warm.

2 Sift the flour into a mixing bowl and stir in the sugar, yeast and salt. Make a well in the center of the dry ingredients and pour in the melted butter and the saffron threads with their soaking liquid. Mash the ricotta cheese with a fork to soften it and add.

3 Stir everything together to make a dough then transfer to a floured work surface and knead by hand for 10 minutes or in an electric mixer with a dough hook fitted for 5 minutes until the dough is smooth and elastic. Place it in an oiled bowl, cover with plastic wrap and leave in a warm place for about 1½–2 hours or until doubled in size.

4 Punch the dough down with your fist and divide it into 12 even-size pieces. Roll each piece of dough into a sausage about 10 inches long and curl each end round as tightly as possible toward the center. Divide the buns between 2 greased baking sheets, cover loosely with oiled plastic wrap and leave in a warm place for about 45 minutes or until doubled in size.

5 Preheat the oven to 425°F. Remove the plastic wrap, brush the buns with the egg yolk glaze and press a raisin into the center of each spiral. Bake for 15 minutes or until golden brown. Transfer to a wire rack to cool.

pancetta and red onion fougasse

Fougasse is a flatbread from Provence that can be sweet or savory. The sweet version, which contains the region's famous candied fruits, traditionally forms the centerpiece of the thirteen desserts served for the Christmas Eve celebrations, while savory fougasse are an everyday bread that is eaten all year round.

SERVES: 8–10

BAKING TIME: 25–30 minutes

1 Tbsp olive oil, plus extra for greasing

1 red onion, peeled and thinly sliced

4 oz pancetta, chopped into small pieces

3½ cups (1 lb 2 oz) bread flour, plus extra if kneading by hand

1½ tsp quick-rise yeast

1 tsp salt

about 1¼ cups warm water

milk, to glaze

1 Heat the olive oil in a skillet and cook the onion over a low heat until softened. Remove the onion from the pan and set aside. Add the chopped pancetta and fry over a medium heat until lightly browned. Drain and set aside.

2 Sift the flour into a mixing bowl and stir in the yeast and salt. Make a well in the center of the dry ingredients and pour in enough water to mix to a soft but not sticky dough – not all the water may be needed so pour in about 1 cup to begin with and add the rest if necessary.

3 Knead the dough for 10 minutes by hand on a lightly floured surface or for 5 minutes in an electric mixer fitted with a dough hook. Add the onion and pancetta and knead for another 1–2 minutes.

4 Put the dough in a greased bowl, cover with plastic wrap and leave in a warm place for about 1 hour or until doubled in size.

5 Remove the dough from the bowl, shape it into a ball and roll it out to a large oval shape. Lift it onto a baking sheet that has been dusted with flour and, using a floured sharp knife or pizza wheel, cut slashes in the dough, starting with a long one down the center and three or four diagonal ones on each side. Stretch the dough with your hands to emphasize the holes.

6 Cover with oiled plastic wrap and leave to prove in a warm place for about 1 hour or until the dough has doubled in size.

7 Preheat the oven to 400°F. Remove the plastic wrap and brush the dough with milk to glaze. Place in the oven and spray a mist of water into the oven before closing the door – this will prevent the dough from forming a crust too quickly and ensure it rises well.

8 Bake for 25–30 minutes or until golden brown and well-risen.

hot cross buns

These sweet spiced, fruity buns with their paste crosses and sugary glaze are traditionally eaten in Britain at Easter on Good Friday but there's no reason you can't enjoy them all year round, with or without their crosses.

MAKES: 12 buns

BAKING TIME: 15 minutes

FOR THE DOUGH

¼ cup (2 oz) butter

3½ cups (1 lb) strong white plain flour, plus extra if kneading by hand

1¼ cups mixed dried fruit

¼ cup (2 oz) superfine sugar

1½ tsp quick-rise yeast

1 tsp ground mixed spice

½ cup warm milk

½ cup warm water

1 egg, beaten

oil, for greasing

FOR THE CROSS PASTE

⅔ cup (3 oz) plain flour

6–8 Tbsp cold water

FOR THE GLAZE

½ cup (4 oz) granulated sugar

6 Tbsp milk

1 To make the dough, rub the butter into the flour and stir in the dried fruit, sugar, yeast and mixed spice.

2 Add the milk, water and beaten egg and mix to make a dough. Knead by hand on a floured surface for about 10 minutes or in an electric mixer fitted with a dough hook for 5 minutes until the dough is smooth and elastic.

3 Transfer the dough to an oiled bowl, cover with plastic wrap and leave in a warm place for 1–2 hours or until doubled in size.

4 Knead the dough again for 1–2 minutes and divide it into 12 even-size pieces. Roll each piece into a ball, flatten the tops and place, well apart, on greased baking sheets. Cover loosely with oiled plastic wrap and leave to rise in a warm place until doubled in size.

5 To make the cross paste, mix the flour with enough cold water to give a smooth paste. Spoon the paste into a disposable pastry bag, snip off the end with scissors and pipe a cross on the top of each bun.

6 Preheat the oven to 400°F and bake the buns for 15 minutes or until golden brown.

7 Make the glaze while the buns are baking by dissolving the sugar with the milk in a saucepan. Bring to the boil and boil for 3 minutes. As soon as the buns come out of the oven, brush them with the glaze and then transfer to a wire rack to cool. Serve warm or cold, split and spread with butter.

TIP The buns are best eaten freshly baked but you can make up the dough the evening before you need them and leave it to rise in a covered bowl overnight in the fridge. Slightly stale buns are delicious split, toasted and served warm with butter.

flatbreads

Pull them apart and dunk them in a tangy dip, wrap them round

a spicy filling, tear off a chunk and use it to scoop up a hot curry

or top them with colorful Mediterranean vegetables and aromatic

herbs – these breads are just made for sharing.

pita bread

Many types of flatbread have been baked for centuries in countries around the eastern Mediterranean and across the Middle East, making them the oldest breads known to mankind. Greek pita is one of the most popular and as the loaves bake, steam creates a fillable cavity inside.

MAKES: 8 pita breads

BAKING TIME: 3–4 minutes
(for each batch of breads)

**3½ cups (1 lb) bread flour,
plus extra for kneading**

1½ tsp salt

1½ tsp quick-rise dried yeast

1¼ cups warm water

2 Tbsp olive oil

1 Tbsp liquid honey

1 Sift the flour into a mixing bowl and stir in the salt and yeast.

2 Mix together the warm water, olive oil and honey. Make a well in the center of the dry ingredients and pour in the honey mixture. Stir to make a smooth dough, adding a little more flour if needed.

3 Turn out the dough onto a floured surface and knead by hand for 10 minutes or in an electric stand mixer with a dough hook on low speed for 5 minutes or until the dough is smooth and elastic.

4 Transfer the dough to an oiled bowl, turning the dough over so it is covered in a thin film of oil. Cover the bowl with plastic wrap and leave in a warm place for about 1½ hours or until the dough has doubled in size.

5 Knock the dough down, transfer it to a floured surface and knead by hand for 1–2 minutes to break up any air bubbles. Divide the dough into 8 even-size pieces and roll each one into a ball. Cover with a dry kitchen towel and set aside to rest for 15 minutes.

6 Roll out each ball of dough to a disk or oval about ¼ inch thick. Arrange the breads in a single layer on well-floured dry kitchen towels and leave in a warm place to rise for about 30 minutes or until doubled in size.

7 Preheat the oven to its highest setting and put a baking stone or baking sheet in the oven to heat. Bake the pita breads in batches by laying two or three at a time on the baking stone or baking sheet, protecting your hand with oven mitts or a thick cloth. Spray the breads with water and bake them for 2–3 minutes until they are starting to brown. If the breads start to brown too much before they are ready (timing will depend on the heat of your oven), lower the temperature. Remove the breads from the oven as soon as they are firm.

8 Transfer the breads to a wire rack as they come out of the oven, covering them with a kitchen towel.

indian paratha

Using ghee (clarified butter) gives these delicious flaky flatbreads a wonderfully rich flavor. They are perfect to serve alongside kebabs or any other spicy foods.

MAKES: 6–8 paratha

BAKING TIME: 12–15 minutes

5 Tbsp ghee, plus a little extra

2¼ cups (9 oz) whole wheat flour

⅓ cup (2 oz) roti flour or all-purpose flour

½ tsp sea salt

1 Melt 3 Tbsp of the ghee. Place both kinds of flour in a large bowl and make a well in the center. Pour the sea salt, ⅔ cup water and the melted ghee into the well and knead well. (Add 1–2 Tbsp more water if necessary.) The dough should be soft. Cover the dough and let it rest for about 1 hour.

2 Divide the dough into 6 or 8 pieces. On a floured surface, roll out each piece to make a thin disk. Place the disks next to each other. Melt 2 Tbsp ghee and brush it over the dough.

3 Melt a little ghee in a skillet or on a griddle and cook the parathas for 2–3 minutes, turning once.

maghreb flatbreads

The Maghreb region of north-west Africa spans Morocco, Tunisia and Algeria and is home to the wonderfully robust meat and vegetable tajines cooked there by the Berber tribes and which take their name from the special pots with funnel-shaped lids they used. Along with couscous, it is traditional to serve flatbreads with a tajine and these will go particularly well with any slow-cooked, preferably spicy, casserole. Like most breads they are best eaten warm, fresh from the oven.

MAKES: 4 flatbreads

BAKING TIME: 15–20 minutes

3⅓ cups (1 lb) bread flour, plus extra if kneading by hand

1½ tsp quick-rise yeast

1 tsp salt

1¼ cups warm water

3 Tbsp olive oil, plus extra for greasing

cornmeal or semolina flour, for sprinkling

1 egg white, lightly beaten

3 Tbsp sesame seeds

2 tsp coarse salt

1 Sift the flour into a mixing bowl and stir in the yeast and salt. Make a well in the center and pour in the water and olive oil. Using a spoon or an electric mixer a dough hook fitted, mix to make a soft, slightly sticky dough.

2 Turn out the dough onto a floured surface and knead by hand for 20 minutes or, if using a food mixer, knead for 5 minutes until smooth and elastic. If kneading by hand, flour the work surface lightly but avoid working too much flour into the dough as this will make it dry. Shape the dough into a ball and place in an oiled bowl. Cover with plastic wrap and leave in a warm place for about 45 minutes or until doubled in size.

3 Line 2 baking sheets with parchment paper and sprinkle each with a dusting of cornmeal or semolina flour. Divide the dough into 4 even-size pieces and flatten each piece into a disk about 6 inches in diameter. Place on the baking sheets, cover with oiled plastic wrap and leave in a warm place for 30–40 minutes or until risen and puffy.

4 Preheat the oven to 425°F. Press indentations in the top of each bread with the floured handle of a wooden spoon or a finger, brush the breads with lightly beaten egg white and sprinkle over the sesame seeds and coarse salt.

5 Bake for 15–20 minutes or until golden and the breads sound hollow when tapped underneath. Serve warm.

lebanese flatbreads

A popular street food in Lebanon is one of these flatbreads sprinkled with a spice mix known as za'tar, a blend of ground sumac, sesame seeds and za'tar, which is a Middle Eastern herb, also known as hyssop, and similar to oregano and marjoram. Sliced tomatoes, onions and shredded lettuce are then piled on the bread and it is rolled up ready to be eaten. Sumac is a widely used spice in Turkey and Lebanon that adds a tart, almost citrusy flavor to meat, chicken and vegetable dishes. Not quite as strong as lemon, sumac was used to give an acidic flavor to dishes before lemons were introduced into the Middle East by the Romans.

MAKES: 12 flatbreads

BAKING TIME: 5–10 minutes

3½ cups (1 lb) bread flour, plus extra for kneading

2 tsp salt

1½ tsp quick-rise dried yeast

1½ tsp granulated sugar

1¼–1½ cups warm water

olive oil, for greasing

1 Sift the flour into a mixing bowl and stir in the salt, yeast and sugar.

2 Make a well in the center of the dry ingredients and pour in the warm water. Mix everything together to make a smooth dough. Transfer the dough to a floured surface and knead it by hand for 10 minutes or in an electric stand mixer for 5 minutes on low speed or until it is smooth and elastic.

3 Put the dough in a bowl lightly rubbed with olive oil and roll the dough over so it is covered in a film of oil. Cover the bowl with a damp kitchen towel and leave in a warm place to rise for about 1½ hours or until doubled in size.

4 Punch the dough down and knead it by hand on a floured surface for

1–2 minutes. Divide it into 12 even-size pieces, roll each piece into a ball, cover with a dry kitchen towel and leave to rest for 20 minutes.

5 Roll each ball of dough to a round about ¼ inch thick, lay the rounds on a dry kitchen towel and leave to rise for 20 minutes until doubled in size.

6 Preheat the oven to 450°F and place 2 large baking sheets in the oven to heat. Brush the top of each dough round lightly with olive oil and slide the rounds onto the baking sheets. Bake for 8–10 minutes golden and puffed. Eat warm or cold on the day they are baked or freeze for up to 1 month and warm in a microwave before serving.

soft flour tortillas

Whether they are made with wheat flour or cornmeal, tortillas accompany just about every dish in Mexico. They are versatile and can be used in a multitude of ways.

MAKES: 10 small tortillas

COOKING TIME: about 10 minutes

1¾ cups (8 oz) all-purpose flour

¼ cup (2 oz) lard, cut into small pieces

1 tsp salt

½ cup warm water

1 Sift the flour into a mixing bowl. Add the lard and rub it in thoroughly. Stir in the salt and add the water, mixing well to make a smooth dough.

2 Turn out onto a floured surface and knead for 2–3 minutes. Wrap the dough in plastic wrap and chill for about 1 hour.

3 Divide the dough evenly into 10 balls and roll out each one on the floured surface, keeping it round, paper-thin and about 6 inches in diameter. As you roll them, stack them with sheets of parchment paper between them.

4 Heat a griddle or large, heavy skillet until very hot. Cook the tortillas, one or two at a time, for 20–30 seconds on each side, until the surface is a light brown and bubbles appear on it. As they are cooked, stack them on a plate and keep them covered and warm under a clean kitchen towel. Serve them warm, preferably straight from the griddle.

TIPS

1 To make spicy tortillas, add a pinch each of coriander, cumin and cinnamon to the flour.

2 To reheat cold tortillas, cook them on a heated griddle for a few seconds on each side, or wrap the whole stack in foil and heat in a 350°F oven for 10–15 minutes.

flatbreads with mint and scallion pesto

Cut into strips or small squares, these flatbreads work really well for canapés, either served plain or topped with shredded prosciutto or cooked chicken, halved cherry tomatoes and olives or capers. The quantities given for the pesto will make more than you need for the breads but store the rest in a covered container in the fridge and use it as a sauce for pasta.

MAKES: 8–10 flatbreads

COOKING TIME: 1–2 minutes each flatbread

FOR THE PESTO

1 cup olive oil

3 cups lightly packed fresh mint leaves

1 bunch of scallions, trimmed and chopped

¾ cup grated Parmesan cheese

⅓ cup pine nuts

4 garlic cloves, peeled and chopped

FOR THE FLATBREADS

2 cups (10 oz) bread flour, plus extra for dusting

2 cups shredded haloumi cheese

1 cup hot water

2 Tbsp olive oil, plus extra for frying

2 Tbsp finely chopped mint

2 Tbsp finely chopped parsley

coarse salt

1 To make the pesto, put half the olive oil in a food processor or pestle and mortar and add the mint leaves, scallions, Parmesan, pine nuts and garlic. Process or grind everything together until smooth. Add the remaining oil a little at a time and process or grind until evenly combined with the remaining ingredients.

2 To make the flatbread, mix the flour with the haloumi cheese, water and oil to make a soft dough. Cover the bowl with plastic wrap and leave the dough to rest for 30 minutes.

3 Turn out the dough onto a floured surface, knead for 1–2 minutes then divide it into 8–10 pieces. Form the pieces into 12-inch lengths and then roll them out flat with a rolling pin.

4 Sprinkle the mint and parsley over the lengths of dough and brush them with the pesto.

5 Heat a little oil in a large, heavy skillet and fry the breads over medium heat for 1–2 minutes until they are golden brown on both sides, turning once.

6 Brush the breads again with the pesto, sprinkle with a little coarse salt and serve warm or cold.

swedish thin bread

In Sweden flatbreads, known as 'tunnbröd, can be hard and brittle or soft enough to wrap round a sandwich filling. This recipe is for making soft breads and in Sweden the dough, which doesn't need to rise, would be rolled out using a 'kruskave,' a special rolling pin with spikes that produces the breads' characteristic pattern of holes. If you don't have a spiked rolling pin, prick the flatbreads all over with a fork.

MAKES: 20 thin breads

BAKING TIME: (bake in pairs): 4–5 minutes for each pair

1½ cups (5 oz) sifted rye flour

1½ cups (5 oz) barley flour, plus extra for dusting

1¼ cups (5 oz) strong white bread flour

1 Tbsp quick-rise dried yeast

2 tsp cumin seeds, crushed

1 tsp salt

2 cups warm milk

1 Preheat the oven to 450°F and place a baking sheet on a middle shelf to heat. Mix the rye flour, barley flour and bread flour in a mixing bowl and stir in the yeast, cumin and salt.

2 Make a well in the center of the dry ingredients and pour in the milk. Work everything together to make a smooth dough.

3 Turn out the dough onto a floured surface and shape it into a disk. Cut it into 20 pieces and shape each one into a ball. Cover the dough balls with a damp kitchen towel.

4 Flour the work surface, preferably with barley flour. Take one ball of dough and roll it out with a smooth rolling pin to make a thin disk.

5 Roll the dough again with a spiked rolling pin until it is well pierced, or prick it all over with a fork. Roll out a second ball of dough in the same way.

6 Place the two rounds of dough on the hot baking sheet and bake for 4–5 minutes, turning them over halfway through cooking time. While the two rounds are baking, roll out two more to go into the oven when the first pair comes out and continue until all the rounds are baked.

7 Cool the flatbreads on a wire rack.

DID YOU KNOW?

Barley, like rye, can grow in harsh conditions and poor soil and has been cultivated since ancient times. Barley's nutritional value is similar to that of wheat although it contains twice as many fatty acids as wheat so has a higher calorie content. Although it can be replaced in a recipe with ordinary wheat flour, barley flour does add a pleasantly nutty flavour to dough so it's worth tracking it down in whole-food stores.

sourdough crispbread

This is a variation on traditional Swedish crispbread that is baked using equal parts of rye sourdough and plain sourdough starters. It is made over two days and a special spiked rolling pin is used to create the distinctive pattern. If you don't have one, a fork makes a practical alternative for piercing the holes.

MAKES: 8 pieces

BAKING TIME: about 15 minutes

¼ cup rye sourdough starter (see recipe on page 34)

¼ cup plain sourdough starter (see recipe on page 33)

¾ cup cold water

2 cups (9 oz) all-purpose flour, plus extra for kneading and rolling

1½ cups (5 oz) rye flour

1½ tsp quick-rise dried yeast

1 tsp coarse salt

ground star anise, crushed fennel or cumin seeds, for sprinkling

DAY 1

1 Put the rye sourdough and plain sourdough starters in the bowl of an electric stand mixer fitted with a dough hook and mix in the water.

2 Sift the all-purpose flour into a separate bowl and stir in the rye flour, yeast and coarse salt, mixing well. Gradually work the flour mixture into the sourdough starters, kneading everything together on low speed until you have a smooth dough.

3 Cover the bowl with plastic wrap and put it in the fridge. Leave the dough to rise overnight.

DAY 2

4 Preheat the oven to 400°F.

5 Knock the dough down and divide it into 8 even-size pieces. Knead each piece until smooth and elastic, adding a little more all-purpose flour if necessary. Roll out each piece of dough using a smooth rolling pin, dusting both the work surface and the top of the dough with flour and turning each piece several times while you are rolling.

6 Sprinkle each piece of dough with ground star anise, crushed fennel or cumin seeds (or another spice of your choice) then roll with a spiked rolling pin or prick all over with a fork.

7 Lift the breads onto a large baking sheet lined with parchment paper and bake for 15 minutes or until the breads are golden brown and dry, turning them over halfway through baking. If, after 15 minutes, they are still a little soft, reduce the temperature to 325°F and bake for a further 5–10 minutes. Eat the crispbreads warm or cold.

DID YOU KNOW?
Traditional Swedish hard bread is round with a hole in the middle, a throwback to the time when the breads were stored on poles under the roof of the house.

langos

This fried bread has been part of Hungary's national cuisine ever since it was introduced into the country by the invading Turks centuries ago. A favorite street food, langos are eaten as a snack, rubbed with garlic and sprinkled with salt, and sometimes caraway seeds or another spice are added to the potato and yeast dough. For a more substantial meal, the langos are topped with sour cream, dill and grated cheese, plus there is a sweet version where the breads are dusted with icing sugar and cinnamon.

MAKES: 8 langos

COOKING TIME: about 4 minutes for each bread

3¼ cups (14 oz) bread flour, plus extra for kneading

1 large potato, boiled, cooled and mashed

1½ tsp quick-rise dried yeast

1 tsp salt

½ tsp ground cumin

1⅓ cups warm water

vegetable oil, for greasing and deep-frying

1 Sift the flour into a mixing bowl and stir in the mashed potato, yeast, salt and cumin.

2 Pour in the warm water and mix everything together to make a dough. Knead by hand on a floured surface for 10 minutes or in an electric stand mixer with a dough hook for 5 minutes.

3 Transfer the dough to an oiled bowl, cover with plastic wrap and leave to rise in a warm place for 1 hour or until doubled in size.

4 Knock the dough down and divide it into 8 even-size pieces. Roll out each piece to a rectangle about 6 inches long.

5 Heat oil for deep-frying to 350°F and deep-fry the breads, in batches, for 2 minutes on each side until golden brown and puffed. Drain on paper towels.

chapati

Chapatis are Indian breads traditionally made from special chapati flour but without a raising agent. Pale brown and quite gritty in texture, chapati flour is made from finely milled whole wheat flour and is available from Indian food stores. Not easy to find unless you have an Asian store near you, it can be replaced with a mixture of whole wheat flour and white bread flour. It's best to use a mix of the two flours, as all white flour will result in leathery chapatis, while breads made solely from whole wheat flour will be too granular.

MAKES: 8 chapati

COOKING TIME: 1–2 minutes for each chapati

½ cup (2½ oz) strong bread flour, plus extra for dusting

½ cup (2½ oz) whole wheat flour

½ tsp salt

about ½ cup warm water

oil, for greasing

melted butter, for brushing

1 Mix the bread flour, whole wheat flour and salt in a mixing bowl. Make a well in the center of the dry ingredients and add enough warm water to make a soft dough.

2 Transfer the dough to a lightly greased board or work surface and knead until it until smooth and pliable.

3 Cover the dough with a damp kitchen towel and leave it to rest for 10 minutes or longer.

4 Divide the dough into 8 even-size pieces and shape each piece into a ball. Take one ball at a time and press it out flat, dusting with flour on both sides. Roll out each ball to a disk 8 inches in diameter, dusting with flour if necessary.

5 Heat a cast-iron skillet until fairly hot. Place one of the dough rounds on the skillet and when brown patches start to appear on the underside and the dough swells, flip it over. Cook for a further 30 seconds, using a spatula to press lightly on the swollen parts as this will help the bread to swell up again. When the bread has golden brown spots on both sides it is ready.

6 Brush the chapati with a little melted butter before removing it from the skillet. Serve warm with Indian food.

naan

Another flatbread from India but, unlike chapatis, naan bread dough has yeast added to it. Traditionally the breads are baked in a special cylindrical 'tandoor' clay oven fired by wood or charcoal, with the naan pressed against the hot sides of the oven and then peeled off when cooked. As most domestic kitchens don't possess such an oven, for practical purposes we've suggested broiling them. The naan won't be quite the genuine article but will still be an excellent accompaniment to curries and other Indian dishes.

MAKES: 6 naan

BAKING TIME: 2–3 minutes for each naan

2 cups (10 oz) strong bread flour, plus extra for kneading and dusting

1 tsp quick-rise dried yeast

1 tsp salt

1 tsp granulated sugar

¼ tsp baking powder

1¾ cups warm water

2½ Tbsp thick plain Greek yogurt

2 Tbsp vegetable oil, plus extra for greasing

melted butter or ghee (see Tip)

1 Sift the flour into a mixing bowl and stir in the yeast, salt, sugar and baking powder.

2 Make a well in the center of the dry ingredients and pour in the warm water. Add the yogurt and vegetable oil and stir everything together.

3 Transfer the dough to a floured surface and knead it by hand for 10 minutes or in an electric stand mixer with a dough hook for 5 minutes until the dough is smooth and elastic.

4 Put the dough in an oiled bowl, turn it over so it is covered in a thin film of oil. Cover the bowl with plastic wrap and leave in a warm place for 1–2 hours or until the dough has doubled in size.

5 Knock the dough down and knead it again for 1–2 minutes by hand on a floured surface. Divide the dough into 6 even-size pieces and roll out each one to a teardrop or oval shape about 8 inches long. Sift a little flour over them.

6 Preheat the broiler to high. Warm a baking sheet under the broiler, place 2 naan on it and broil for 2–3 minutes until they are golden, light and fluffy. Broil the remaining breads in the same way.

7 Brush the naan with melted butter or ghee and serve hot.

TIP Ghee is a type of clarified butter from India that, although similar to western clarified butter, is made using a different type of cream. This is simmered until all the moisture has evaporated and the milk solids begin to turn brown, resulting in a butter that has a nutty, caramel-like flavor and a longer shelf life. Ghee also burns at a higher temperature than ordinary butter, making it particularly suitable for frying. For flavored naan breads, sprinkle poppy seeds, chopped garlic mixed with chopped cilantro, black onion seeds or sesame seeds over the surface of the breads and press the topping into the dough before broiling.

focaccia

It's been claimed that focaccia originates from ancient Greece but today we associate these soft, open-textured flatbreads with Italy. Served plain, the breads make an excellent accompaniment to a platter of antipasti made up of a selection of cured meat, cheese and roasted vegetables. Serve the focaccia warm straight from the oven to enjoy it at its best.

MAKES: 2 focaccia

BAKING TIME: 10–15 minutes

3½ cups (1 lb 2 oz) unbleached strong bread flour or Italian '00' flour, plus extra for dusting

1½ tsp quick-rise dried yeast

1½ tsp salt

1¼ cups warm water

3 Tbsp olive oil, plus extra for greasing

chopped oregano, or rosemary or thyme leaves, for sprinkling (optional)

1 Sift the flour into the bowl of an electric stand mixer fitted with a dough hook and stir in the yeast and salt.

2 Add the water and work on low speed to make a dough, kneading for about 5 minutes or until the dough is smooth and elastic.

3 Put the dough in an oiled bowl, cover with plastic wrap and leave to rise in a warm place for about 1½ hours or until doubled in size.

4 Knock the dough down and transfer it to a floured surface. Cut it in half with a floured sharp knife.

5 Brush two rimmed baking sheets with olive oil. Roll out each piece of dough thinly on a floured surface and lift onto the baking sheets. Cover with dry kitchen towels and leave to rise in a warm place for 30–45 minutes or until doubled in size.

6 Preheat the oven to 475°F. Dimple the tops of the focaccia with a floured finger or wooden spoon handle and brush with olive oil. If wished, sprinkle over chopped oregano, or rosemary or thyme leaves. Bake in the oven for 10–15 minutes or until the focaccia are golden brown.

focaccia with fleur de sel and rosemary

Many cooks regard fleur de sel – 'flower of salt' in French – as the finest sea salt there is and combined with rosemary it makes a lovely crunchy and aromatic topping for this classic Italian flatbread. Harvested by hand, it is collected by workers who scrape off the top layer of salt before it sinks in the large salt pans. Most comes from Brittany, particularly around the town of Guérande, but the salt is also produced in Portugal, Spain, the Camargue region of the south of France and now also in Brazil.

MAKES: 1 loaf

BAKING TIME: 20–25 minutes

4⅓ cups (1 lb 5 oz) unbleached plain white bread flour, plus a little extra if kneading by hand

2 tsp quick-rise yeast

2 tsp table salt

1½ cups warm water, plus ⅓ cup for brushing

1 tsp liquid honey

2 Tbsp extra virgin olive oil, plus extra for greasing

FOR THE TOPPING

2 Tbsp fleur de sel or coarse sea salt

1 Tbsp finely chopped fresh rosemary

1 Sift the flour into a large mixing bowl and stir in the yeast and 1 tsp table salt. Pour in 1½ cups water, add the honey and 1 Tbsp olive oil and mix to make a soft dough.

2 Knead by hand on a lightly floured surface for 5 minutes or in an electric mixer fitted with a dough hook for 3–4 minutes. Shape the dough into a ball and place in an oiled bowl. Cover with plastic wrap and leave in a warm place for 1½ hours or until doubled in size.

3 Lightly oil a large baking sheet. Knock the dough down, knead for a further 1 minute then lift it onto the baking sheet. Gradually stretch out the dough with your hands until it covers the sheet, letting the dough relax in between stretches.

4 Push a toothpick into each corner of the dough and cover loosely with a clean kitchen towel. Leave to rise in a warm place for 45 minutes.

5 Preheat the oven to 475°F. Stir the remaining table salt and olive oil into ⅓ cup warm water. Dimple the surface of the dough by pressing a floured finger into it at regular intervals and then brush all over with the oil and salt mixture. You probably won't need all the mixture but the dough should be well moistened, especially around the edges.

6 Sprinkle over the fleur de sel and rosemary and bake for 20–25 minutes or until the focaccia is golden brown and sounds hollow when tapped on the bottom. Slide onto a wire rack and leave to cool for 10 minutes before slicing or tearing.

focaccia stuffed with spinach and taleggio

In Italy millers grade their wheat flour by '0' ratings, a single zero indicating that the flour is quite coarse, similar to semolina, while triple-zero flour is much finer. Everyday flour is graded '00' and can be golden or white in color – the golden being used for making pasta, while the white is for breads such as this focaccia. White '00' flour is lower in protein than normal bread flour so produces a crisper crust but if you can't track it down, ordinary bread flour can be substituted.

SERVES: 6–8

BAKING TIME: 30–35 minutes

3½ cups (1 lb 2 oz) Italian '00' flour, plus extra if kneading by hand

1½ tsp quick-rise yeast

1 tsp salt

about 1 cup warm water

3 Tbsp olive oil, plus extra for greasing and brushing

5 oz Taleggio cheese, rind removed and cut into dice

4 oz mozzarella, sliced

2 cups baby spinach leaves

½ cup drained sun-blushed or sun-dried tomatoes, coarsely chopped

1 Mix the flour, yeast and salt together in a bowl. Whisk together the water and olive oil and pour into the dry ingredients, mixing to make a soft dough that comes away from the sides of the bowl – you may need to add a little extra water to achieve the correct consistency.

2 Turn the dough out onto a floured surface and knead by hand for 10 minutes or do this in an electric mixer fitted with dough hook for 5 minutes until the dough is smooth and elastic.

3 Transfer the dough to an oiled bowl, cover with plastic wrap and leave to rise in a warm place for 1½–2 hours or until doubled in size.

4 Knock the dough down and divide it in half. Roll out each piece to a 10-inch disk. Lift one piece of dough onto a lightly oiled baking sheet and top with the Taleggio, mozzarella, baby spinach leaves and sun-blushed tomatoes, spreading everything out in an even layer. Dampen the edges of the dough and lift the second piece on top, pinching and crimping the edges together to seal.

5 Cover with oiled plastic wrap and leave in a warm place to rise for about 30 minutes until slightly risen.

6 Preheat the oven to 400°F. Uncover the focaccia and press dimples all over the top with a floured finger or the handle of a wooden spoon. Brush with olive oil and bake for about 30–35 minutes or until golden brown. Eat warm.

tear and share wrap breads

Equally good wrapped around any filling that takes your fancy from chili and curries to roasted vegetables or a crisp, colorful salad, these versatile flatbreads are also good for tearing into pieces and scooping up dips. They can also be served as an accompaniment to a rich meat stew or a Moroccan tajine instead of potatoes or rice. In summer, cook them on the grill rather than in a nonstick skillet, if you prefer.

MAKES: about 10 wrap breads

BAKING TIME: 3–4 minutes for each wrap bread

4 cups (1 lb 2 oz) plain white flour, plus extra for kneading

1 Tbsp chopped fresh cilantro

2 tsp baking powder

1 tsp paprika

1 tsp ground cumin

1 tsp salt

5 Tbsp olive oil

about 1 cup water

1 Sift the flour into a bowl and stir in the cilantro, baking powder, paprika, cumin and salt.

2 Add the olive oil and enough water to bind the ingredients together to make a fairly firm and not sticky dough. Knead until smooth on a lightly floured surface and divide the dough into 10 even-size pieces.

3 Roll out one piece of dough to a very thin disk, about 8 inches in diameter, keeping the remaining pieces covered loosely with oiled plastic wrap. Heat a nonstick skillet until very hot and cook the disk of dough for a couple of minutes on each side or until brown spots appear on the surface.

4 Repeat with the remaining pieces of dough to make 10 wrap breads, piling up the ones you've cooked and keeping them covered with a kitchen towel dampened with warm water to keep them soft, while you cook the rest. Serve warm.

pizza

In 1889, to celebrate a visit by the Italian king Umberto I and his queen, Margherita of Savoy, Raffaele Esposito baked his version of the Italian flag and served it at the restaurant he ran with his wife, the Pizzeria Brandi. Topping a sheet of dough with crushed tomatoes (red), mozzarella cheese (white) and basil leaves (green), he christened his creation 'pizza Margherita' in honour of the Queen. From Naples, pizza crossed the Atlantic to New York City. The first pizzeria being opened in 1905 by Gennaro Lombardi in Spring Street, SoHo.

MAKES: 4 pizzas

BAKING TIME: about 10 minutes

FOR THE PIZZA DOUGH

3½ cups (1 lb 2 oz) unbleached bread flour, please extra for kneading

1½ tsp quick-rise dried yeast

1 tsp salt

1 cup warm water

1 Tbsp olive oil, plus extra for greasing

SUGGESTED TOPPINGS

tomato sauce

sliced or shredded mozzarella cheese

sliced mushrooms, chopped bell peppers, sliced tomatoes, pitted black olives

prosciutto slices, arugula, radicchio or basil leaves, to serve

1 To make the pizza dough, sift the flour into a bowl and stir in the yeast and salt. Make a well in the center of the dry ingredients and pour in the warm water. Add the olive oil and mix to make a dough.

2 Turn out the dough onto a floured surface and knead it by hand for 10 minutes or in the bowl of an electric stand mixer fitted with a dough hook on low speed for 5 minutes, or until the dough is smooth and elastic.

3 Put the dough in an oiled bowl, cover it with plastic wrap and leave to rise in a warm place for 1½ hours or until doubled in size.

4 Knock the dough down and knead it by hand on a floured surface for 1–2 minutes. Divide the dough into 4 even-size pieces and roll out each piece to a thin round the size of a large dinner plate and about ¼ inch thick. Cover the rounds with oiled plastic wrap or a dry kitchen towel and leave to rise for 15 minutes.

5 Preheat the oven to its highest setting or 475°F and put baking sheets or a pizza stone in the oven to heat.

6 Spread tomato sauce over the pizza crusts, leaving a border round the edge, and top with sliced or shredded mozzarella cheese and other ingredients of your choice, such as sliced mushrooms, chopped bell peppers, sliced tomatoes and pitted black olives.

7 Bake for 10 minutes or until the pizza crusts are crisp and golden brown. Remove them from the oven, top with prosciutto slices, arugula, radicchio or basil leaves and serve immediately.

pissaladière

SERVES: 6

BAKING TIME: about 50 minutes (for
the onions), 25–30 minutes (for baking the
pissaladière)

FOR THE BASE

**1½ cups (7 oz) bread flour,
plus extra for kneading**

2 tsp quick-rise yeast

1 tsp salt

1 tsp granulated sugar

⅔ cup warm water

**1 Tbsp olive oil, plus extra for
greasing**

FOR THE TOPPING

**4 Tbsp olive oil, plus extra for
drizzling**

**4 large onions, peeled and thinly
sliced**

2 cloves garlic, peeled and crushed

2 tsp fresh thyme leaves

2 tsp chopped fresh rosemary leaves

2 tomatoes, peeled and chopped

**1 can (2 oz) anchovy fillets, drained
and halved lengthways**

about 36 small pitted black olives

Provence's answer to Italian pizza, the yeast dough base is traditionally topped with fried onions, herbs, tomatoes, anchovies and black olives. It is important to cook the onions very slowly over a gentle heat in the olive oil so they become soft and mellow rather than brown and crisp.

1 To make the base, sift the flour into a mixing bowl and stir in the yeast, salt and sugar. Make a well in the center of the dry ingredients and pour in the water and olive oil. Mix to a dough then turn out onto a floured surface and knead for 5 minutes or until smooth and no longer sticky.

2 Place the dough in an oiled bowl, cover with plastic wrap and leave in a warm place for about 1 hour or until doubled in size.

3 While the dough is rising, make the topping. Heat the olive oil in a large skillet, add the onions and cook over a very low heat for about 10 minutes until softened but not browned. Stir in the garlic, thyme and rosemary, cover the skillet and cook gently for 30 minutes or until the onions are meltingly soft, stirring occasionally. Remove the lid from the skillet, add the tomatoes and cook for a further 10 minutes or until any liquid from the tomatoes has evaporated.

4 Preheat the oven to 425°F. Knock the dough down and knead for 1–2 minutes before rolling it out and pressing in a thin even layer into a greased shallow 13- x 9-inch baking pan.

5 Spread the dough with the onion mixture and arrange the halved anchovies over the top in a diagonal lattice pattern. Place an olive in each diamond and bake for 25–30 minutes or until the dough is golden. Drizzle with a little extra olive oil and serve straight from the oven.

shaped breads

From plaited cranberry and walnut bread and crunchy, salt-sprinkled pretzels tied in a bow, to half-moon croissants, long thin grissini and brioche or cottage loaves with their topknot of dough, challenge yourself and have lots of fun in the process by creating the eye-catching breads we've included here.

challah rolls

This Jewish bread, traditionally eaten on the Sabbath, was first made in the Middle Ages by Jews living in Central Europe and from there it spread to the West as communities migrated. The sweet dough is enriched with eggs and it is traditionally shaped into elaborate braids with large loaves having up to 12 strands of dough twisted together. Such a large number of strands is impractical for making small rolls so in this variation the dough is shaped into knots.

MAKES: 12 rolls

BAKING TIME: 10–12 minutes

5 cups (1 lb 8 oz) bread flour, plus extra for kneading

1½ tsp quick-rise dried yeast

1 tsp salt

1 cup warm water

3 eggs, beaten

⅓ cup (3 oz) unsalted butter, melted and cooled

3 Tbsp liquid honey

oil, for greasing

beaten egg, to glaze

1 Sift the flour into a mixing bowl and stir in the yeast and salt. Make a well in the dry ingredients and pour in the warm water. Add the eggs, melted butter and honey and mix to a make |a soft but not sticky dough.

2 Knead the dough on a lightly floured surface by hand for 10 minutes or in an electric stand mixer fitted with a dough hook on low speed for 5 minutes or until it is smooth and elastic.

3 Put the dough in an oiled bowl and turn it over so the dough is covered with a thin film of oil. Cover the bowl with plastic wrap and leave it in a warm place for about 1½ hours or until the dough has doubled in size.

4 Punch the dough down with your fist, then cover the bowl with plastic wrap and leave it to rise again until doubled in size – this will take about 45 minutes.

5 Punch the dough down again, turn it out onto a floured surface and knead by hand for 1–2 minutes. Divide the dough into 12 even-size pieces using a floured sharp knife and roll each piece into a sausage shape, about 8 inches long. Tie each one into a loose knot and divide between two greased baking sheets, leaving room for the rolls to rise.

6 Cover the rolls with oiled plastic wrap and leave in a warm place for about 30 minutes or until doubled in size.

7 Preheat the oven to 425°F. Brush the rolls with beaten egg to glaze and bake for 10–12 minutes or until golden brown. Slide them off the baking sheet onto a wire rack to cool.

pretzels

Various legends have evolved down the centuries as to the origins of pretzels, one being that around 610 AD a young monk in central Europe was preparing unleavened bread for Lent. At that time people prayed with their arms folded across their chests with their hands on opposite shoulders and the monk came up with the idea of shaping the dough to represent this.

MAKES: 6 pretzels

BAKING TIME: 10–15 minutes

2½ cups (12 oz) bread flour, plus extra for kneading

1 Tbsp light soft brown sugar

1 tsp quick-rise dried yeast

1 tsp salt

1 cup warm milk

FOR THE TOPPING

1 egg, beaten with 2 Tbsp milk

coarse sea salt

1 Sift the flour into a bowl and stir in the sugar, yeast and salt. Make a well in the center of the dry ingredients and pour in the warm milk, stirring to form a dough.

2 Knead the dough by hand on a floured surface for 10 minutes or in an electric stand mixer fitted with a dough hook on low speed for 5 minutes, or until the dough is smooth and elastic.

3 Put the dough in an oiled bowl, cover with plastic wrap and leave in a warm place to rise for 1 hour or until doubled in size.

4 Knock the dough down, knead it by hand for 1–2 minutes on a floured surface and then divide it into 6 even-size pieces with a floured sharp knife. Roll out each piece of dough with the palms of your hands to form thick sausages shapes. Cover with a damp kitchen towel and let them rest for 10 minutes.

5 Roll out the sausages of dough again with your hands until they are long and about ½ inch thick. Twist the ends round and loop one under the other to make the traditional pretzel 'knot,' dampening the ends of the dough to fix them in place.

6 Bring a large saucepan of water to the boil and simmer the pretzels one at a time for 10 seconds each. Lift them out with a slotted spoon so the water drains off.

7 Preheat the oven to 425°F. Put the pretzels on baking sheets lined with parchment paper and brush them with the beaten egg and milk. Sprinkle with coarse sea salt.

8 Bake for 10–15 minutes or until the pretzels are crisp and a rich golden brown. Eat the pretzels freshly baked – they are particularly good spread with a little mustard.

brioche

A light, sweet bread with a soft crumb from France that can be eaten plain, spread with butter and jam or drizzled with honey. Brioche comes in different shapes but the classic loaf, brioche à tête, is baked in a fluted mold with a smaller ball of dough on top.

SERVES: 8 brioche

BAKING TIME: 20 minutes

1¾ cups (8 oz) strong white plain flour, plus extra for kneading

1 Tbsp superfine sugar

1½ tsp quick-rise yeast

½ tsp salt

2 large eggs, beaten

¼ cup (2oz) unsalted butter, melted

2 Tbsp warm water

sunflower oil, for greasing

milk, to glaze

1 Sift the flour into a bowl and stir in the sugar, yeast and salt. Pour in the beaten eggs, melted butter and warm water and beat with a wooden spoon until the ingredients are well mixed. Press the mixture together with your hands to make a soft, sticky dough.

2 Transfer the dough to a floured surface and knead for about 10 minutes by hand or for 5 minutes in an electric mixer fitted with a dough hook until smooth and elastic.

3 Grease a large bowl with oil, put the dough in it and cover the bowl with plastic wrap. Leave in a warm place for about 1 hour or until the dough has doubled in size.

4 Knock back the dough with your knuckles, take it out of the bowl and knead on a lightly floured surface for 1–2 minutes. Cut off about one quarter of the dough and shape the rest into a smooth ball. Put this into a lightly oiled 4-cup fluted brioche silicone mold or pan.

5 Make a depression in the center of the dough in the mold. Shape the remaining smaller piece into a smooth ball and place it in the depression, pressing it down lightly.

6 Cover the dough with greased plastic wrap and leave it to rise in a warm place until puffy and doubled in size. Remove the plastic wrap and brush the dough with milk to glaze.

7 Preheat the oven to 450°F. Set the mold or pan on a baking sheet and bake for 20 minutes until golden brown and crusty on top. If after 15 minutes the brioche is sufficiently browned, cover the top with a sheet of foil. Turn the brioche out and place on a wire rack to cool. Serve warm or cold, either plain or toasted and s pread with butter and jam or drizzled with honey.

danish pastries

MAKES: 8 pastries

BAKING TIME: 10–12 minutes

FOR THE DOUGH

1⅔ cups (8 oz) bread flour, plus extra for kneading and rolling out

1 Tbsp superfine sugar

2 tsp quick-rise dried yeast

½ tsp salt

⅔ cup (5 oz) butter

4 Tbsp warm water

1 egg, beaten, plus extra for glazing

oil, for greasing

SUGGESTED FILLINGS
APPLE AND RAISINS

2 Tbsp butter

1 apple, peeled, cored and grated

¼ cup raisins

2 Tbsp superfine sugar

½ tsp ground cinnamon

ALMOND

⅓ cup ground almonds

2 Tbsp superfine sugar

2 tsp lemon juice

a little beaten egg

TO DECORATE

a little beaten egg, to glaze

Despite their name, these pastries owe their origins to Austrian bakers who, in 1850, came from Vienna to Copenhagen to work. Unfamiliar with local methods they introduced their own ways of making light and flaky pastries. To this day Danes still call these pastries Wienerbrød (Vienna Bread).

1 To make the dough, sift the flour into a mixing bowl and stir in the sugar, yeast and salt. Rub in 2 Tbsp of the butter and stir in the warm water and beaten egg. Mix to a firm dough then knead by hand on a lightly floured surface for 5 minutes. Wrap in plastic wrap and chill for 30 minutes.

2 Roll out the dough on a floured surface to a rectangle and spread the remaining butter over two-thirds of it. Fold the unbuttered third of dough over half the buttered section then fold the remaining buttered section over the top.

3 Seal the edges by pressing with the rolling pin and roll out the dough again to a long thin rectangle. Fold into thirds again, wrap in plastic wrap and chill for 30 minutes. Repeat the rolling, folding and chilling process twice more.

4 To make the apple and sultana filling, melt the butter in a saucepan and stir in the apple, raisins, sugar and cinnamon. Cook for 1 minute then set aside to cool.

5 To make the almond filing, mix the ground almonds and sugar together, then stir in the lemon juice and enough beaten egg to form a stiff paste.

6 Roll out the dough to a large rectangle and cut into 8 even-size squares. Spoon a little filling of your choice into the center of each square and fold the corners in over the filling (or form the dough into any other shapes you prefer). Place on a greased baking sheet, cover with oiled plastic wrap and leave in a warm place for about 20 minutes to rise.

7 Preheat the oven to 425°F. Brush the pastries with beaten egg to glaze and sprinkle with chopped nuts, if wished. Bake for 10–12 minutes or until golden brown. Leave to cool completely before drizzling some of the pastries with glaze.

brown beer bread

Use a dark beer to make this delicious loaf as it will give it a richer flavor and deeper color. Caraway seeds add a touch of warm spice but poppy seeds, dill seeds or the tiny black seeds in cardamom pods, crushed in a pestle and mortar, would be equally good.

MAKES: I loaf

BAKING TIME: 35–40 minutes

1½–1¾ cups (7–9 oz) bread flour, plus extra if kneading by hand

1⅔ cups (7 oz) strong whole wheat bread flour

1 Tbsp dark muscovado sugar

1 Tbsp caraway seeds, plus extra for sprinkling

1½ tsp quick-rise yeast

1 tsp salt

1 cup brown ale or a similar dark beer, warmed

½ cup warm water

2½ Tbsp sunflower oil, plus extra for greasing

beaten egg, to glaze

1 Sift 1½ cups (7 oz) white flour into a mixing bowl and stir in the whole wheat flour, sugar, caraway seeds, yeast and salt.

2 Pour in the beer, water and oil and mix until the dough starts to come together. Knead by hand on a floured surface for 10 minutes or in an electric mixer fitted with a dough hook for 5 minutes or until the dough is smooth and elastic, working in the remaining white flour as necessary.

3 Transfer the dough to an oiled bowl, cover with plastic wrap and leave in a warm place for about 1½ hours or until doubled in size.

4 Knock the dough down and divide it into 3 even-size pieces. Roll each piece to a 14-inch long rope and braid them together, dampening and pressing the ends lightly together to seal.

5 Lift the braid onto a greased baking sheet, cover with oiled plastic wrap and leave to rise again until doubled in size.

6 Preheat the oven to 375°F. Remove the plastic wrap and brush the top of the braid with beaten egg. Sprinkle with a few more caraway seeds and bake for 35–40 minutes or until the bottom of the loaf sounds hollow when tapped. Transfer to a wire rack to cool.

tomato braid

This loaf is flavored with sun-blushed tomatoes that can be bought bottled in oil or loose from the deli counter of your local supermarket. A brighter more attractive red than dark brown sun-dried tomatoes, they also have a sweeter, juicier flavor.

MAKES: 1 loaf

BAKING TIME: 40 minutes

3½ cups (1 lb 2 oz) bread flour, plus extra for dusting

1½ tsp quick-rise dried yeast

1 tsp salt

1¼ cups warm water

1 jar sun-blushed tomatoes in oil, drained and chopped, and oil reserved

coarse sea salt

freshly ground black pepper

1 Sift the flour into a mixing bowl and stir in the yeast and salt. Whisk the warm water with 4 Tbsp oil from the tomatoes and add to the flour mixture with half the chopped tomatoes, stirring to make a dough.

2 Knead the dough by hand on a floured surface for 10 minutes or in an electric stand mixer fitted with a dough hook on low speed for 5 minutes or until the dough is smooth and elastic.

3 Put the dough in an oiled bowl, cover with plastic wrap and leave in a warm place to rise for 1–2 hours or until doubled in size.

4 Punch the dough down and knead it by hand on a floured surface for 1–2 minutes.

5 Divide the dough into 3 even-size pieces and, with the palms of your hands, roll out each one to a sausage shape about 1-inch thick. Braid the lengths of dough together and bring the ends round to form a ring, dampening the ends of the dough to seal the ring. Lift this carefully onto a baking sheet lined with parchment paper.

6 Brush the dough with oil from the tomatoes and press the remaining chopped tomatoes evenly into the dough. Sprinkle with coarse sea salt and coarsely ground black pepper.

7 Cover the braid loosely with plastic wrap and leave it to rise in a warm place for about 45 minutes or until doubled in size.

8 Preheat the oven to 425°F. Remove the plastic wrap and bake the loaf for 20 minutes. Reduce the oven temperature to 375°F and bake for a further 20 minutes or until the bread sounds hollow when tapped on the base. Slide the loaf off the baking sheet onto a wire rack to cool.

croissants

One of the pleasures of a trip to France is sitting in the sunshine outside a bustling café breakfasting on a steaming cup of coffee and a rich, buttery croissant.

MAKES: 12 croissants

BAKING TIME: 15–20 minutes

3½ cups (1 lb 2 oz) bread flour, plus extra for kneading and rolling out

⅓ cup (3 oz) superfine sugar

2 tsp quick-rise dried yeast

2 tsp salt

1¼ cups warm water

1⅓ cups (11 oz) cold unsalted butter

oil, for greasing

beaten egg, to glaze

1 Sift the flour into a mixing bowl and stir in the sugar, yeast and salt. Add the water and mix to make a fairly stiff dough – this is easiest if done in an electric stand mixer fitted with a dough hook on low speed for about 5 minutes.

2 Turn out the dough onto a lightly floured surface, shape it into a ball, dust it with flour, wrap in plastic wrap and chill for 1 hour.

3 Roll out the dough to a rectangle about ½ inch thick. Shape the butter into a rectangle by flattening it with a rolling pin between two sheets of plastic wrap and place it on the dough so it covers the bottom two-thirds of the dough and comes almost to the edges.

4 Fold the top third of the dough down to cover one-third of the butter. Cut off the exposed piece of butter without cutting into the dough and lift this piece of butter on top of the dough that you have folded down. Fold the bottom half of the dough up. Seal in the butter by pressing the dough edges together with the rolling pin. Wrap the dough in plastic wrap and chill for 1 hour.

5 Roll out the dough again to a rectangle about ½ inch thick. Fold up one-third of the dough from the bottom and then fold the top third down over it. Wrap in plastic wrap and chill again for 1 hour. Repeat this rolling, folding and chilling twice more.

6 Put the dough in a clean plastic bag, seal the bag loosely and leave the dough in the fridge overnight to rise a little.

7 Roll out the dough again to a rectangle about ¼ inch thick and trim the edges neatly. Cut the rectangle in half lengthways then cut each strip into 6 triangles. Starting at the longest side of each triangle, roll up each triangle toward its point, pressing the point down lightly. Place on two or three baking sheets lined with parchment paper, leaving space for the croissants to rise. Bend the pointed ends inwards to make a crescent shape if wished.

8 Cover with oiled plastic wrap and leave the croissants to rise in a warm place for about 1½ hours or until doubled in size.

9 Preheat the oven to 400°C. Brush the croissants with beaten egg to glaze and bake for 15–20 minutes or until a rich golden brown. Eat warm.

cheddar and sage sticks

A strong Cheddar adds plenty of bite to this bread, making it a good choice for baguette-style sandwiches. Rye flour adds its own deep, rich flavor but it's a good idea to mix it with ordinary bread flour so the crumb of the baked loaves is not as dense as it would be if all rye flour was used.

MAKES: 2 sticks

BAKING TIME: 20 minutes

2¼ cups (8 oz) strong rye flour

1⅔ cups (8 oz) bread flour, plus extra if kneading by hand and for dusting

1 cup shredded Cheddar cheese

1 Tbsp finely chopped fresh sage

1½ tsp quick-rise yeast

1 tsp superfine sugar

1 tsp salt

about 1¼ cups warm water

oil, for greasing

1 In a large bowl, mix together the rye flour, bread flour, grated cheese, sage, yeast, sugar and salt.

2 Stir in enough warm water and mix to make a soft dough – you may find you need slightly less or slightly more water to achieve the correct consistency.

3 Transfer the dough to a lightly floured surface and knead by hand for 10 minutes or in the bowl of an electric mixer fitted with a dough hook for 5–6 minutes until smooth and elastic.

4 Place the dough in an oiled bowl, cover with plastic wrap and leave in a warm place for about 1½ hours or until doubled in size.

5 Brush a large baking sheet lightly with oil. Knock down the dough and knead it by hand on a floured surface for 1–2 minutes. Divide the dough in half and shape each piece into a stick about 12 inches long.

6 Lift the sticks onto the baking sheet, spaced well apart, and leave them to rise in a warm place for about 1 hour or until doubled in size. Score the top of each stick in a crisscross pattern using a sharp knife dusted with flour.

7 Preheat the oven to 425°F. Place a roasting pan of hot water on the bottom shelf of the oven with the loaves on the baking sheet on a middle shelf and bake for 20 minutes or until the sticks sound hollow when tapped underneath.

cranberry and walnut plait

Instead of cranberries, you could use blueberries to make this impressive braided loaf and replace the walnuts with pine nuts, pecans or hazelnuts. Strip the thyme leaves off their stalks before adding them to the dough rather than chopping the whole sprigs as, although the leaves are soft and aromatic, the stalks can be unpleasantly woody.

SERVES: 10–12

BAKING TIME: 40 minutes

3½ cups (1 lb 2 oz) bread flour, plus extra if kneading by hand

1½ tsp quick-rise yeast

1 tsp salt

1 tsp superfine sugar

4 Tbsp olive oil, plus extra if kneading by hand

1¼ cups warm water

oil, for greasing

⅓ cup dried cranberries or ½ cup frozen cranberries, defrosted

¼ cup chopped walnuts

2 tsp fresh thyme leaves

milk, to glaze

1 Sift the flour into a mixing bowl and stir in the yeast, salt and sugar. Whisk 4 Tbsp olive oil into the warm water and add to the flour mixture, stirring to make a dough.

2 Knead by hand on a floured surface for about 10 minutes, rubbing oil on your hands as you knead to prevent the dough from becoming dry, or knead in an electric mixer with a dough hook fitted for about 5 minutes or until the dough is smooth and elastic.

3 Place the dough in an oiled bowl, cover with plastic wrap and leave in a warm place to rise for 1–2 hours. Punch the dough down and knead again for 1–2 minutes, working in the cranberries, chopped walnuts and thyme.

4 Divide the dough into three even-size pieces and roll each piece to a sausage about 1½ inches thick. Braid the three sausages together, dampening and pinching the ends together and lift carefully onto a greased baking sheet. Cover loosely with oiled plastic wrap and leave to rise in a warm place for about 45 minutes or until the braid has doubled in size.

5 Preheat the oven to 400°F. Remove the plastic wrap and brush the loaf with milk to glaze.

6 Bake for 20 minutes then reduce the oven temperature to 350°F and bake for a further 20 minutes or until golden brown and the loaf sounds hollow when tapped underneath.

cottage loaf

This country-style loaf with its glistening golden crust and turban-style top-knot makes a good family loaf for everyday eating. You can also shape the dough into a dozen individual rolls, which will take less time to rise and bake.

MAKES: 1 loaf

BAKING TIME: 20–25 minutes

3⅓ cups (1 lb) bread flour, plus extra if kneading by hand

1½ tsp quick-rise yeast

1 tsp salt

⅔ cup warm milk

⅔ cup warm water

¼ cup (2 oz) butter, melted

oil, for greasing

TO GLAZE

1 egg, beaten

3 Tbsp poppy seeds

1 Sift the flour into a bowl and stir in the yeast and salt. Make a well in the center and add the milk, water and melted butter, and mix together to make a fairly sticky dough.

2 Knead on a floured surface for about 10 minutes by hand or in an electric mixer with a dough hook fitted for about 5 minutes until the dough is smooth and elastic and no longer sticky.

3 Transfer the dough to an oiled bowl, cover with plastic wrap and leave to rise in a warm place for about 1½ hours or until doubled in size.

4 Knock the dough down and knead again for 1–2 minutes. Cut off one quarter of the dough and roll this into a ball with your hands. Shape the larger piece of dough into a ball and place on a baking sheet lined with parchment paper.

5 Sit the small ball of dough on top. Dip the handle of a wooden spoon in flour and push the handle through the center of the two balls of dough right the way down to the baking sheet. Carefully lift out the spoon handle, cover the loaf loosely with oiled plastic wrap and leave to rise in a warm place for about 45 minutes or until doubled in size.

6 Preheat the oven to 425°F. Remove the plastic wrap, brush the loaf with beaten egg and sprinkle over the poppy seeds. Bake in the oven for 20–25 minutes or until golden and the loaf sounds hollow when tapped on the bottom. Slide it onto a wire rack to cool.

grissini

Also known as bread sticks, grissini can be made in different thicknesses and lengths and the unbaked dough sprinkled with coarse salt or aromatic seeds, as you prefer. The sticks are great as nibbles with drinks or make short versions to serve with party dips.

MAKES: 20 long or 40 short breadsticks

BAKING TIME: 30 minutes

5 cups (1 lb 8 oz) bread flour, plus extra for kneading

2 tsp quick-rise dried yeast

2 tsp salt

2 cups warm water

2 Tbsp olive oil, plus extra for greasing

beaten egg, to glaze

coarse salt, sesame and poppy seeds or other seeds, for sprinkling

1 Sift the flour into a bowl and stir in the yeast and salt. Make a well in the center of the dry ingredients and pour in the warm water. Add the olive oil and work everything together to make a dough.

2 Knead the dough on a floured surface by hand for 10 minutes or in an electric stand mixer fitted with a dough hook for 5 minutes on low speed or until the dough is smooth and elastic.

3 Put the dough in an oiled bowl, cover it with plastic wrap and leave in a warm place to rise for 60 minutes or until doubled in size.

4 Knock the dough down and knead it by hand on a floured surface for 1–2 minutes. Divide the dough into small pieces and roll out each piece with the palms of your hands to a thin stick. Lay the sticks on baking sheets lined with parchment paper, leaving space between them so they can rise.

5 Brush the sticks with beaten egg and sprinkle over coarse salt, sesame and poppy seeds or other seeds of your choice. Cover with plastic wrap and set aside in a warm place to rise for a further 60 minutes.

6 Preheat the oven to 400°F and bake the sticks for about 30 minutes or until they are golden brown and feel dry.

'stick' bread

Here's a fun idea for a camping trip or even a backyard party: these breads should be wrapped around a stick and roasted on an open fire. Try wrapping the stick bread dough around a half-grilled sausage then continue cooking to make sausage bread.

MAKES: 4–6 sticks

BAKING TIME: a few minutes

1 cup (4½ oz) plain flour

1 tsp baking powder

½ tsp salt

⅓ cup plus 2 Tbsp water

4–6 wooden skewers, soaked in water for 1 hour

1 Stir together the flour, baking powder and salt in a bowl. Add the water and mix into a dough. Work the dough until it is no longer sticky, adding more flour if necessary.

2 Dry the skewers, then roll the dough into a ¼-inch thick sausage shapes and wrap them around the skewers in a spiral fashion. Bake over a hot fire until they feel done.

Try to make the dough about ¼ inch thick. It will then be evenly baked and won't burn on the outside before the inside, closest to the stick, is done. Bake over coals until it feels done.

iced fruit crown

SERVES: 12

BAKING TIME: 35–45 minutes

3 cups (14 oz) bread flour, plus extra if kneading by hand and for rolling out

2 Tbsp butter, diced

3 Tbsp superfine sugar

1½ tsp quick-rise yeast

1 tsp salt

4 Tbsp warm milk

about ¾ cup warm water

oil, for greasing

FOR THE FILLING

1 Tbsp butter, melted

½ cup raisins

⅓ cup currants

⅓ cup raisins

¼ cup (2 oz) light muscovado sugar

3 Tbsp chopped almonds

1 tsp ground cinnamon

¼ tsp grated nutmeg

TO DECORATE

6 Tbsp confectioners' sugar

about 1 Tbsp cold water

extra raisins and chopped almonds

An eye-catching sweet bread that's packed with dried fruits, nuts and spice and decorated with a final flourish of drizzled white icing.

1 Sift the flour into a bowl and rub in the butter. Stir in the superfine sugar, yeast and salt. Make a well in the center of the dry ingredients and pour in the milk and enough of the water to mix to a soft dough

2 Transfer the dough to a lightly floured surface and knead it by hand for about 10 minutes or in an electric mixer.

3 Place the dough in an oiled bowl, cover with plastic wrap and leave in a warm place to rise for about 1½–2 hours or until doubled in size.

4 Punch the dough down then knead it again for 1–2 minutes before rolling it out on a floured surface to a 15- × 8-inch rectangle.

5 To make the filling, brush the dough with melted butter, leaving a ¾-inch border on one long side. Mix together the raisins, currants, raisins, muscovado sugar, almonds, cinnamon and nutmeg and spread over the buttered area of the dough.

6 Brush the unbuttered border with water and roll up the dough tightly from the opposite side, pressing the dampened strip against the roll to seal it.

7 Shape the roll into a ring and lift onto a baking sheet lined with parchment paper, placing the join underneath. Slash the dough several times with a sharp, floured knife, cutting halfway through the roll. Cover with oiled plastic wrap and leave to rise in a warm place until doubled in size.

8 Preheat the oven to 400°F. Remove the plastic wrap and bake the crown for 35–45 minutes or until it is golden and sounds hollow when tapped on the base, covering it with foil when the top is brown enough.

9 Slide the crown off the baking sheet onto a wire rack and leave to cool. Mix the confectioners' sugar with enough cold water to make a smooth icing. Spoon the icing into a disposable pastry bag, snip off the end and drizzle the icing over the crown. Stud with extra raisins and chopped almonds. Leave until the icing has set before serving.

flavored breads

Bread might be 'the staff of life' but that doesn't mean it has to be boring! Try working saffron and pumpkin, feta and tomatoes, figs and pecan, or zucchini and marmalade into your dough and you'll see what we mean.

pumpkin, saffron and rosemary bread

Pumpkin and saffron give this loaf a rich golden glow, echoing the colors of autumn when pumpkins are season. It's an ideal loaf to make for a Halloween celebration – serve it warm with mugs of chunky soup or grilled sausages.

MAKES: 1 loaf

BAKING TIME: 30–35 minutes

9 oz peeled and seeded pumpkin

½ tsp saffron threads

⅓ cup plus 2 Tbsp boiling water

2½ cups (12 oz) bread flour, plus extra if kneading by hand

1 tsp salt

2 Tbsp finely chopped fresh rosemary leaves

1 tsp quick-rise yeast

oil, for greasing

1 Cut the pumpkin into 1-inch cubes and steam for 7–10 minutes or until tender. Drain on a plate lined with paper towel so any moisture in the pumpkin can be absorbed by the paper, mash and set aside to cool.

2 Crumble the saffron threads into a bowl and pour the boiling water over them. Set aside to soak for 10 minutes or until the water becomes warm.

3 Sift the flour and salt into a mixing bowl, stir in the chopped rosemary and yeast and add the pumpkin and saffron with its soaking liquid. Mix together to make a slightly sticky dough then transfer to a floured surface and knead for about 10 minutes until smooth and elastic. Alternatively, make the dough in an electric mixer fitted with a dough hook, kneading it for 5–6 minutes.

4 Shape the dough into a ball and place it in an oiled bowl. Cover with plastic wrap and leave in a warm place to rise for about 1½ hours or until it has doubled in size.

5 Knock the dough down, knead by hand on a floured surface for 1–2 minutes and shape it into a ball. Lift the dough onto a lightly oiled baking sheet, cover with oiled plastic wrap and leave to rise for about 30 minutes or until doubled in size.

6 Preheat the oven to 400°F. Cut a diamond pattern in the top of the loaf using a floured sharp knife and bake for 30–35 minutes or until the bread is golden brown and sounds hollow when tapped on the base.

feta, tomato and walnut loaf

The salty tang of feta cheese combined with the sweetness of cherry tomatoes will make this savory loaf a favorite with lovers of Mediterranean food. It can be served warm or cold either on its own or as an accompaniment to an antipasti platter of cold meats and olives or mixed seafood such as marinated shrimp, mussels and baby squid.

SERVES: 6

BAKING TIME: 40–45 minutes

4 eggs

2¾ cups (12 oz) plain flour

2 Tbsp butter, melted and cooled

2 Tbsp sunflower oil, plus extra for greasing

2 tsp baking powder

6 cherry tomatoes, halved

1 cup grated Parmesan cheese

1 cup diced feta cheese

½ cup chopped walnuts

1 tsp fresh thyme leaves

salt and freshly ground black pepper

1 Preheat the oven to 350°F. In a large mixing bowl, beat the eggs with a fork until light and frothy. Sift in the flour, add the melted butter, sunflower oil and baking powder and beat until smooth and all the ingredients are evenly combined.

2 Add the cherry tomatoes halves to the mixture with the Parmesan, feta, walnuts and thyme, season with salt and freshly ground black pepper and stir until mixed in.

3 Spoon the mixture into a greased 9- x 5-inch loaf pan, spread the top level and set the pan on a baking sheet.

4 Bake for 40–45 minutes or until a skewer pushed into the center of the loaf comes out clean. Leave the loaf to cool in the pan for 10 minutes before turning it out. Serve warm or cold.

rosemary potato bread

Sporting a crisp potato and rosemary top, these rolls will be the talking point at any gathering. For a variation, try different herbs in the dough and on the topping.

MAKES: 12 rolls

BAKING TIME: 20–25 minutes

FOR THE DOUGH:

3 ¼ cups (14 oz) all-purpose flour

2 tsp quick-rise dried yeast

2 Tbsp olive oil

1 Tbsp chopped rosemary leaves

1½ cups warm water

FOR THE TOPPING:

1 medium potato (7 oz), sliced very thinly

2 Tbsp olive oil

1 Tbsp fresh rosemary leaves

Salt and black pepper

1 Sift the flour into a large bowl and sprinkle on the yeast, a pinch of salt, the oil and rosemary. Make a well in the center and pour in the water (you may need a little less or more). Mix well, then turn out onto a floured surface. Knead very thoroughly to a smooth dough. Place it in a bowl and let it rise for about 30 minutes in a warm place, until it has doubled in size.

2 Preheat the oven to 425°F.

3 Knead the dough again thoroughly on the floured surface. Shape the dough into 12 balls and flatten them slightly.

4 Blanch the potato slices for 1–2 minutes in boiling water. Dip quickly into cold water and drain. Place the potato slices on top of the rolls and press down slightly. Brush with olive oil and sprinkle rosemary leaves on top. Season with salt and pepper.

5 Place the rosemary potato bread rolls on an oiled baking sheet and bake for 20–25 minutes until golden brown.

TIP These rolls can be frozen and reheated in the oven when required.

cinnamon-raisin bread

This fruity loaf is enriched with milk and is so good it can be eaten unbuttered. It's also delicious toasted and spread with honey or jam.

MAKES: 1 large loaf (about 16 slices)

BAKING TIME: 30 minutes

3¾ cups (1 lb) strong whole wheat bread flour

2 tsp cinnamon

1½ tsp salt

⅔ cup raisins

3 Tbsp superfine sugar

2 tsp quick-rise dried yeast

1 cup semi-skimmed milk, plus extra for glaze

¼ cup (2 oz) unsalted butter

1 egg, lightly beaten

1 Grease and lightly flour a 9- x 5-inch loaf pan. Sift the flour, cinnamon and salt into a large mixing bowl, tipping in any leftover bran. Stir in the raisins, sugar and yeast and make a well in the center.

2 Gently heat the milk and butter in a small saucepan, and when the butter has melted, pour it into the well. Add the beaten egg and mix together to make a soft dough.

3 Turn the dough out onto a lightly floured surface and knead until the dough feels elastic, about 10 minutes. Shape the dough and place it in the loaf pan. Cover with a clean kitchen towel and leave to rise in a warm place. After an hour it should have doubled in size.

4 Near the end of the rising time, preheat the oven to 425°F. Uncover the loaf, brush it with the milk and bake for about 30 minutes, until it sounds hollow when you tap the base. Turn it out to cool on a rack. It can be kept, wrapped in foil, for 2–3 days.

TIP
You can vary the flavor by using other dried fruit, such as chopped, dried apricots.

black currant quick bread

The fruity (but not too sweet) black currants in this unusual quick bread combine with the fresh tang of mint to make a summer treat to be proud of. When black currants are plentiful, make a batch of loaves and freeze them for up to 2 months.

MAKES: I large loaf

BAKING TIME: 1¼ hours

2¾ cups (12 oz) self-rising flour

I tsp baking powder

4 Tbsp unsalted butter, in small cubes

½ cup (3½ oz) light muscovado sugar

I cup fresh black currants

3 Tbsp chopped fresh mint

⅔ cup orange juice

1 Preheat the oven to 350°F. Grease a 9- x 5-inch loaf pan and line it with parchment paper.

2 Sift the flour and baking powder into a bowl. Rub in the butter until the mixture resembles fine bread crumbs. Stir in the sugar and form a well in the center.

3 Drop the black currants and fresh mint into the well, then add the orange juice. Gradually stir all the ingredients together. The mixture should be quite wet, so add more orange juice if necessary.

4 Pour the mixture into the loaf pan, smooth the top and bake for I hour and 15 minutes until the loaf feels firm to the touch. If, after about 50 minutes, the loaf seems to be browning too fast, loosely cover with a piece of foil.

5 Leave the bread to cool in the pan for about 5 minutes, then turn it out onto a rack. It is best left overnight before eating. It will keep in an airtight container for up to 3 days.

TIPS

I For a Christmas treat, substitute cranberries for the black currants and ½ cup chopped pecans for the mint. Add ½ tsp cinnamon for festive flavor.
2 If you prefer blueberries, use them in place of the black currants.

DID YOU KNOW?

Black currants are known to contain four times as much vitamin C as oranges.

fig and pecan malted bread

A hearty tea bread that's bursting with interesting textures and flavors. The loaf freezes well so it makes a good standby for when friends and family come to call. To freeze, wrap the cold loaf in a freezer bag and seal it tightly. When ready to serve, defrost the loaf completely and then refresh it in a hot oven for 5 minutes before slicing.

MAKES: I loaf

BAKING TIME: 25–30 minutes

3½ cup (I lb 2 oz) malted-grain bread flour, plus extra if kneading by hand

2 Tbsp light muscovado sugar

I½ tsp quick-rise yeast

I tsp salt

I¼ cups warm water

2 Tbsp sunflower oil, plus extra for greasing

I¼ cups chopped dried figs

¾ cup chopped pecans

1 Tip the flour into a mixing bowl and stir in the sugar, yeast and salt. Make a well in the center of the dry ingredients and pour in the water and oil. Mix to make a soft dough then turn out onto a lightly floured surface and knead by hand for 10 minutes or in an electric mixer fitted with a dough hook for 5 minutes or until the dough is smooth and elastic.

2 Add the chopped figs and pecans and knead again until mixed in. Place the dough in an oiled bowl, cover with plastic wrap and leave to rise in a warm place until doubled in size.

3 Knock the dough down and knead again for 1–2 minutes. Shape it into an oval and place in a greased 9- x 5-inch loaf pan, pressing the dough down into the corners of the pan. Cover with oiled plastic wrap and leave in a warm place to rise until doubled in size.

4 Preheat the oven to 425°F. Remove the plastic wrap, set the loaf pan on a baking sheet and bake for 25–30 minutes or until golden brown and the base of the loaf sounds hollow when tapped. If the loaf browns too quickly before it is baked, cover the top with a sheet of foil.

5 Leave the loaf to cool in the pan for 5 minutes before turning it out onto a wire rack to cool. Serve warm or cold.

sour cream and chive loaf

A simple bread made a bit more special by the tangy addition of sour cream and snipped fresh chives. The loaf goes well with salads and soups or it can be sliced to make sandwiches for a picnic or the family lunch boxes.

MAKES: I loaf

BAKING TIME: 35 minutes

2–2½ cups (10–12 oz) bread flour, plus extra if kneading by hand

2 Tbsp superfine sugar

1½ tsp quick-rise yeast

1 tsp salt

½ cup sour cream, at room temperature

¼ cup warm water

1 egg, beaten

3 Tbsp butter, melted and still warm but not hot

2 Tbsp snipped fresh chives

oil, for greasing

extra beaten egg, to glaze

1 Sift 2 cups (10 oz) flour into a mixing bowl and stir in the sugar, yeast and salt.

2 Add the sour cream, warm water, beaten egg, melted butter and chives and mix to make a soft dough, adding as much of the remaining flour as needed.

3 Transfer to a floured surface and knead by hand for 10 minutes or in an electric mixer fitted with a dough hook for 5 minutes or until the dough is smooth and elastic.

4 Place the dough in an oiled bowl, cover with plastic wrap and leave to rise in a warm place for about 1 hour or until doubled in size.

5 Knock down the risen dough, knead again for 1–2 minutes and shape into a loaf. Place in a greased 9- x 5-inch loaf pan, cover with oiled plastic wrap and leave to rise again in a warm place for 30–40 minutes or until it has doubled in size.

6 Preheat the oven to 375°F. Glaze the top of the loaf with extra beaten egg. Set the pan on a baking sheet and bake for about 35 minutes or until the loaf sounds hollow when tapped on the base. Turn out and cool on a wire rack.

onion and oregano loaf

Serve this full-flavored loaf with cheese, cold chicken and ham or as an accompaniment to grilled sausages. Sauté the onions slowly over a low heat so they become meltingly soft and golden rather than over a high heat that will turn them brown and crisp.

MAKES: I loaf

BAKING TIME: about 50 minutes

FOR THE FILLING

2 Tbsp extra virgin olive oil

2 medium onions, peeled and finely sliced

I Tbsp finely chopped fresh oregano

I Tbsp tomato paste

FOR THE BREAD DOUGH

3½ cups (I lb 2 oz) bread flour, plus extra if kneading by hand and dusting

I½ tsp quick-rise yeast

I tsp salt

I cup warm water

¼ cup extra virgin olive oil, plus extra for greasing

I Tbsp black onion seeds

1 To make the filling, heat the olive oil in a saucepan and fry the onions over a gentle heat for about 20 minutes or until they are soft and golden, covering the pan with a lid after 5 minutes to stop the onions from browning, and stirring them occasionally. Stir in the chopped oregano and tomato paste and set aside to cool.

2 To make the bread dough, sift the flour into a bowl and stir in the yeast and salt. Add the water and olive oil and mix to make a soft dough. Turn out the dough onto a floured surface and knead by hand for about 10 minutes or in an electric mixer fitted with a dough hook until smooth and elastic. Put the dough in an oiled bowl, cover with plastic wrap and leave it to rise in a warm place for 1–2 hours or until it has doubled in size.

3 Punch down the dough to knock out any air trapped in it and knead on a floured surface for 1–2 minutes. Flatten the dough with your hands and spoon the onion mixture into the center. Wrap the dough around the filling, dampening the edges and pressing them together to seal and shape into a ball or an oval.

4 Lift the dough onto a greased baking sheet with the join underneath, cover loosely with oiled plastic wrap and leave to rise in a warm place for about 45 minutes or until doubled in size.

5 Preheat the oven to 425°F. Remove the plastic wrap and make diagonal cuts across the top of the loaf with a floured knife. Dust the top of the loaf lightly with flour and bake for 30 minutes or until it is golden brown and sounds hollow when tapped on the base. Transfer to a wire rack to cool.

spiced pumpkin bread

This quick bread is moist enough to eat without butter because pumpkin has a high water content. It's rich in color and delicious as an afternoon treat or tucked into a lunch pail.

MAKES: I large loaf

BAKING TIME: 50–60 minutes

3 cups peeled, diced pumpkin

½ cup liquid honey

½ cup raisins

1⅓ cups (5½ oz) self-rising whole wheat flour

1⅓ cups (5½ oz) self-rising white flour

2 tsp ground allspice

⅔ cup (5½ oz) unsalted butter, in small cubes

1 Tbsp pumpkin seeds

1 Preheat the oven to 350°F and line a 9- × 5-inch loaf pan with parchment paper.

2 Boil the pumpkin in a little water for about 10 minutes, until it is tender. Drain it thoroughly and mash until smooth. Add all but 2 tsp of the honey and the raisins and mix well.

3 Sift the two flours and the spice into a bowl, and tip in any bran left in the sieve. Add the butter and rub it in with your fingers until the mixture is the texture of bread crumbs.

4 Add the pumpkin mixture and mix well with a wooden spoon. Spoon the batter into the prepared pan and smooth the surface, before sprinkling it with the pumpkin seeds.

5 Bake the loaf for 50–60 minutes until it is well risen, firm to the touch and golden brown. Let it cool for 10 minutes, then turn it out onto a cooling rack. Glaze the top with the remaining honey and serve warm.

TIPS

1 Try using butternut squash in place of the pumpkin.
2 Add ½ cup chopped pitted dates and 3 Tbsp chopped walnuts in place of the raisins, sprinkling the top with chopped walnuts.
3 Instead of a loaf, make 12 muffins, using a muffin pan and baking for 20–25 minutes.

german fruit and nut bread

There's no added fat in this deliciously fruity bread – all its fat comes from the nuts. Sliced thickly for snack time, or toasted and buttered for breakfast, it has a rich, moist texture and keeps well.

MAKES: I round loaf

BAKING TIME: 30–40 minutes

3 cups (14 oz) strong white bread flour

2 tsp quick-rise dried yeast

Grated zest of ½ lemon

½ tsp salt

½ cup coarsely chopped dried apricots

½ cup coarsely chopped dried pears

½ cup coarsely chopped pitted prunes

¼ cup coarsely chopped dried figs

¼ cup chopped mixed nuts, such as almonds, hazelnuts or cashews

I cup warm water

1 In a large bowl, mix the flour, yeast, lemon zest and salt. Add the chopped fruits and nuts and mix well. Stir in the water and mix by hand to make a soft, heavy dough.

2 Turn the dough out onto a floured surface and knead 10 minutes until it feels pliable.

3 Put the dough into a lightly greased bowl, cover it with a damp kitchen towel and leave in a warm place to rise for 1½–2 hours or until it has doubled in size.

4 Turn the dough out onto the floured surface and knock it back. Gently knead it into a ball and place it on a greased baking sheet. Cover it with the damp kitchen towel again and leave to rise in a warm place for about an hour.

5 Near the end of the rising time, preheat the oven to 400°F. Uncover the loaf and bake for 30–40 minutes until it is nicely browned and sounds hollow when you tap the base. Cover it loosely with foil if it browns too quickly. Transfer it to a rack and leave to cool. It will keep for up to 5 days.

TIP

You can make spicy fruit buns by substituting 2 tsp ground mixed spice and ¼ tsp freshly grated nutmeg for the lemon zest. After the first rising, divide the dough evenly into 12 balls. Space them well apart on a greased baking sheet and leave to rise for 45 minutes, by which time they should have doubled in size. Bake for 25 minutes.

cherry, blueberry and walnut bread

An unusual loaf made from a mix of whole wheat, rye and white bread flours with dried cherries and blueberries added to the dough for extra texture and flavor.

MAKES: 1 loaf

BAKING TIME: about 25 minutes

1½ cups (6 oz) strong whole wheat bread flour

1¼ cups (6 oz) bread flour, plus extra if kneading by hand and 1 Tbsp for dusting

1 cup (4 oz) strong rye flour

⅔ cup chopped walnuts

½ cup dried cherries

⅓ cup dried blueberries

1½ tsp quick-rise yeast

1 tsp salt

1 ⅓ cups warm water

2 Tbsp walnut oil or light olive oil

1 Tbsp liquid honey

1 tsp lemon juice

oil, for greasing

1 Mix the whole wheat, white bread and rye flours together in a mixing bowl and stir in the walnuts, dried cherries, dried blueberries, yeast and salt.

2 Using a fork, whisk together the warm water, walnut oil or light olive oil, honey and lemon juice. Make a well in the center of the flour mixture and pour in the warm water mixture. Stir to make a soft dough then either knead by hand on a surface dusted with flour for 10 minutes or in an electric mixer fitted with a dough hook for 5 minutes, until smooth and elastic.

3 Transfer the dough to an oiled bowl, cover with plastic wrap and leave it in a warm place to rise for about 1½ hours or until doubled in size.

4 Punch the dough down and knead it by hand for 1–2 minutes before shaping into an 7-inch ball or an oval. Place on an oiled baking sheet, cover with oiled plastic wrap and leave to rise again until doubled in size.

5 Preheat the oven to 400°F. Remove the plastic wrap from the dough and, using a sharp knife dipped in flour, cut a slash through the top of it. Dust with the remaining 1 Tbsp white bread flour.

6 Bake the loaf for about 25 minutes or until well browned and the loaf sounds hollow when tapped underneath. Cool on a wire rack.

zucchini and marmalade tea bread

If you grow your own zucchini and are looking for innovative ways of using up a bumper crop, this recipe is sure to be a hit with all the family. On its own grated zucchini can be – let's face it – a bit dull but mixed with a little marmalade it transforms the taste of this tea bread.

MAKES: I loaf

BAKING TIME: I hour

I Tbsp butter, melted, for greasing

2¼ cups (10 oz) plain flour, plus extra for dusting

½ tsp baking soda

½ tsp baking powder

½ tsp ground cinnamon

¼ tsp grated nutmeg

⅔ cup vegetable oil

½ cup (5 oz) superfine sugar

⅓ cup orange marmalade

2 large eggs

2 small zucchini, grated

2 Tbsp demerara sugar

I Preheat the oven to 350°F. Brush a 9- x 5-inch loaf pan with the melted butter and dust with flour.

2 Sift the flour, baking soda, baking powder, cinnamon and nutmeg into a mixing bowl. In another bowl, whisk together the oil, sugar, marmalade and eggs until evenly combined. Stir in the grated zucchini, then add the dry ingredients and fold in until everything is just combined.

3 Pour the batter into the loaf pan, spreading the top with a blunt knife so the surface is smooth. Sprinkle with the demerara sugar.

4 Bake for I hour or until a skewer pushed into the center of the loaf comes out clean. Cool in the pan for 20 minutes before turning out onto a wire rack to cool completely. Serve plain or spread with extra marmalade.

TIP The older the bananas are, the sweeter they will be. Don't discard bananas that have turned brown – this is the perfect way to use them.

african banana bread

Banana bread is a traditional favorite, this banana loaf from from Namibia, in Southern Africa, is ideal for coffee time, a picnic or for adding to a lunch pail. Enjoy it warm and fresh or let it cool then spread with butter.

MAKES: I loaf

BAKING TIME: I hour

I cup (8 oz) packed light brown sugar

½ cup (4 oz) butter, softened

2 eggs, beate

I tsp vanilla

I½ cups (6 oz) all-purpose flour

½ cup (I¾ oz) whole wheat flour

2 tsp baking powder

½ tsp grated nutmeg

I tsp cinnamon

Pinch of salt

⅓ cup raisins

4 Tbsp chopped pecans

6 very ripe bananas, peeled and mashed

1 Preheat the oven to 350°F and grease a 9- x 5-inch loaf pan.

2 Beat the butter and sugar in a mixing bowl until light and fluffy. Add the eggs and vanilla, beating the mixture thoroughly.

3 Mix together the dry ingredients and stir them into the egg mixture. Add the mashed bananas, raisins and pecans and mix thoroughly.

4 Spoon the mixture into the loaf pan and bake for about I hour or until a skewer inserted in the center of the loaf comes out clean. Cool in the pan for 10 minutes, then place on a rack to cool.

english teacakes

Lightly toasted and spread with a little butter and jam, these typically English treats are a favorite at an afternoon tea.

MAKES: 10 teacakes

BAKING TIME: 10–15 minutes

1⅔ cups (8 oz) strong white bread flour

2 cups (8 oz) strong wholemeal bread flour

1 tsp salt

¼ cup (2 oz) unsalted butter, in small cubes

2 Tbsp superfine sugar

½ cup currants

½ cup raisins

2 tsp quick-rise dried yeast

½ tsp cinnamon

1¼ cups warm semi-skimmed milk, plus extra for glazing

1 Sift both flours and the salt into a large bowl, tipping in any bran left in the sieve.

2 Rub in the butter, then stir in the sugar, currants, raisins, yeast and cinnamon.

3 Make a well in the center and pour in the milk, adding more if necessary, to make a soft dough.

4 Turn the dough onto a floured surface and knead it for about 10 minutes, until it feels smooth and elastic. Put in a lightly greased bowl, cover with a kitchen towel and leave it to rise in a warm place for about 1–2 hours, or until it has doubled in size.

5 Turn it out again onto the floured surface and knock it back. Knead for 2–3 minutes, then cut it into 10 even-size pieces, shaping each piece into a ball.

6 Space the balls evenly on 2 greased baking sheets and cover them with clean kitchen towels. Leave them to rise for 30–60 minutes, until they feel puffy.

7 Toward the end of the rising time, preheat the oven to 425°F. Brush the tops of the teacakes with milk and bake them for 10–15 minutes. When they are nicely browned, let them cool on a rack. Serve warm or split and toast them. They are best eaten the same day, but will keep for a day or two.

quick breads

The process of rising and proving yeast doughs could never be described as 'quick' but the good news is not every dough has to contain yeast to make it rise. If you need a speedy loaf for the family's tea, look no further than the recipes in this chapter. With bacon and chilli cornbread, granary fruit bread, Irish soda bread and many more – you'll be spoilt for choice.

irish soda bread

In Ireland the most common type of soda bread is made just from flour, baking soda, salt, and water or milk but, as with so many traditional recipes, over the years bakers have added their own special twists. Raisins, caraway seeds, molasses and cream are just some of the things that are now included in the basic mix.

MAKES: 1 loaf

BAKING TIME: 35–40 minutes

4 cups (1 lb 3 oz) all-purpose flour

2 Tbsp granulated sugar

1 tsp salt

1 tsp baking powder

5 Tbsp butter

1 cup raisins

1 cup half-and-half cream

1 cup milk

1 egg, beaten

1 Preheat the oven to 425°F.

2 Sift the flour into a bowl and stir in the sugar, salt and baking powder. Cut up the butter into small pieces and work it into the flour with your fingertips until the mixture resembles fine breadcrumbs.

3 Add the raisins followed by the cream, milk and beaten egg. Mix everything together quickly into a dough, turn it out onto a floured board and shape it into a ball. Flatten into a 9- to 10-inch round and lift it onto a baking sheet lined with parchment paper. Cut a diagonal cross in the top of the dough with a floured sharp knife.

4 Bake in the oven for 15 minutes then reduce the temperature to 425°F and bake for a further 20–25 minutes or until the loaf is brown and sounds hollow when tapped underneath. The bread is best served warm.

bacon and chilli cornbread

The batter can be baked in a large pan and served cut into squares or you can make individual muffin-sized corn breads as I've done here. If you prefer to use a large pan, line a 9-inch square pan with parchment paper, spoon in the batter and bake for 25–30 minutes at 400°F, or until a skewer comes out clean.

MAKES: 12 cornbreads

BAKING TIME: 15 minutes (for individual cornbreads), 25–30 minutes (if using a 9-inch pan), plus frying time for bacon and onions.

1 Tbsp oil

4 slices bacon, snipped into small pieces with kitchen scissors

3 scallions, finely chopped

¾ cup corn kernels, well-drained if canned

½ tsp red pepper flakes

3 cups (13 oz) plain flour

1½ cups (8 oz) fine cornmeal

1 Tbsp superfine sugar

1 tsp salt

1 tsp baking powder

½ tsp baking soda

1¾ cups buttermilk

2 eggs, beaten

1 Tbsp light corn syrup

1 Tbsp butter, melted

1 Heat the oil in a small skillet and fry the bacon until it is crisp and lightly browned. Remove from the skillet and set aside. Add the scallions and fry for 1–2 minutes. Stir in the corn kernels and red pepper flakes then remove the skillet from the heat and leave to cool.

2 Preheat the oven to 400°F. Sift the flour into a bowl and stir in the cornmeal, sugar, salt, baking powder and baking soda. Add the corn mixture, pour in the buttermilk, eggs, corn syrup and melted butter and stir well until all the ingredients are evenly combined.

3 Line a 12-cup muffin pan with paper liners and spoon in the batter. Bake for 15 minutes or until a skewer pushed into the center of one of the corn breads comes out clean. Serve warm.

oat break bread with chives

This unusual bread is best eaten straight from the oven. The combination of oats and chives makes the bread the ideal accompaniment to a wedge of strong cheese and a few cherry tomatoes or radishes.

MAKES: 12 rolls

BAKING TIME: 18–20 minutes

1 ¼ cups (7 oz) rolled oats

¾ cup milk

1 Tbsp olive oil

1 ¼ cups (5 oz) all-purpose flour

⅓ cup chopped chives

2 tsp baking powder

1 tsp granulated sugar

½ tsp salt

milk and rolled oats for the topping

1 Preheat the oven to 425°F.

2 Put the oats in a bowl and pour over the milk and olive oil. Let the mixture stand for 5 minutes so the oats swell up.

3 In another bowl, mix together the flour, chives, baking powder, sugar and salt. Stir into the oat mixture until evenly mixed then work everything together with your hands to make a dough.

4 Divide the dough into 12 even-size pieces and roll each one into a ball. Put them on a greased baking sheet so they are just touching each other. Brush the tops with milk and sprinkle with extra oats.

5 Bake the bread in the oven for 18–20 minutes or until golden brown.

6 Cover with a dry kitchen towel and serve as soon as the bread is cool enough to handle, pulling the individual rolls apart.

goat cheese, roasted pepper & oregano cornbread

You can roast your own red pepper or buy a ready-roasted one either in a jar or from the deli counter to save time. If roasting your own, set the pepper on a sheet of foil and roast it on all sides until the skin chars and blackens. Wrap the foil around the pepper and leave until it is cool enough to handle before unwrapping, stripping off the skin, removing the seeds and chopping the flesh.

MAKES: 1 cornbread

BAKING TIME: 20–25 minutes

oil, for greasing

1¼ cups (5 oz) plain flour

1 cup (5 oz) fine cornmeal

½ cup grated Parmesan cheese

1 Tbsp baking powder

1 Tbsp superfine sugar

½ tsp salt

½ tsp freshly ground black pepper

1 cup buttermilk

2 eggs, beaten

2 Tbsp extra virgin olive oil

1 Tbsp chopped fresh oregano

1 roasted red bell pepper, seeded and coarsely chopped

2 oz firm goat cheese, broken or chopped into small chunks

1 Preheat the oven to 400°F. Lightly oil a deep, rimmed baking sheet or shallow roasting pan measuring about 10 x 6 inches and line it with parchment paper.

2 Mix the flour, cornmeal, grated Parmesan, baking powder, superfine sugar, salt and pepper together in a bowl. Add the buttermilk, beaten eggs, olive oil and oregano and beat well until evenly combined.

3 Spoon the mixture into the prepared pan, spreading it to the edges in an even layer. Scatter over the chopped red bell pepper and goat cheese and bake for 20–25 minutes or until the corn bread is risen and golden brown.

4 Serve warm on transfer to a wire rack to cool.

TIP If using a red pepper from a jar, drain it well on paper towel before adding to the dough.

banana bread

This fruit loaf is the perfect way to use up any overripe bananas that lie languishing in the fruit bowl because they've turned brown. Unsurprisingly as bananas grow so prolifically in the West Indies, recipes for this bread are part of the indigenous cuisines of the Caribbean islands and there are many variations, some adding nuts and spices, other being left plain. The important thing is that the bananas are very ripe so they have a sweet flavor, otherwise the bread will be dull and bland.

MAKES: 1 loaf

BAKING TIME: 1 hour

⅓ cup (3 oz) butter, softened

¾ cup (6 oz) light muscovado sugar

2 large, overripe bananas

2 large eggs

1¼ cups (5 oz) plain white flour

1 cup (4 oz) plain whole wheat flour

1 tsp baking soda

1 tsp ground cinnamon

¼ tsp freshly grated nutmeg

⅓ cup chopped pecans

oil, for greasing

1 Preheat the oven to 350°F. In a mixing bowl, beat the butter until creamy and then gradually beat in the sugar.

2 Peel the bananas and cut them into chunks. Place in a blender with the eggs and blend until smooth.

3 Mix together the plain and whole wheat flours, baking soda, cinnamon and nutmeg.

4 Stir the blended bananas and eggs into the creamed butter and sugar alternately with the dry ingredients until evenly mixed together. Finally stir in the pecans.

5 Oil a 9- x 5-inch loaf pan and line it with parchment paper. Pour the mixture into the pan and bake for 1 hour or until a skewer pushed into the center of the loaf comes out clean. If after about 45 minutes the top of the loaf is sufficiently brown, cover it with foil for the remaining cooking time.

6 Cool the loaf in the pan for 30 minutes before turning it out onto a wire rack to cool completely. Serve the bread cut into slices, either plain or spread with butter.

yogurt fruit bread

Oats, dried fruits and yogurt make a healthy combination in this unusual but easy to prepare loaf. Lingonberries grow in Sweden's ancient forests and they are a staple part of that country's national cuisine. Lingonberry jam is served with everything from meatballs and pancakes to crisp breads and toast but if you can't find it, cranberry sauce works equally well.

MAKES: 1 loaf

BAKING TIME: 50–60 minutes

2 cups (9 oz) all-purpose flour

1½ cups plain yogurt

1 cup (5 oz) rolled oats

1 cup chopped dried apricots, raisins, sunflower seeds or nuts

¾ cup (3 oz) rye flour

1 tsp salt

1 tsp baking soda

⅓ cup plus 2 Tbsp cranberry sauce or lingonberry jam

butter, for greasing

1 Preheat the oven to 400°F.

2 Mix the plain flour, yogurt, oats, dried fruit, seeds or nuts, rye flour, salt and baking soda together in a bowl then add the sauce or jam.

3 Pour the mixture into a buttered and floured 9- x 5-inch loaf pan, set it on a baking sheet and bake in the oven for 50–60 minutes or until a metal skewer pushed into the center of the loaf comes out clean.

4 Cool the loaf in the pan for 15 minutes before turning it out onto a wire rack to cool completely.

TIP The bread can be made as individual rolls in a 12-cup muffin pan. Store the baked cooled rolls in the freezer for an energy-boosting breakfast or mid-morning snack. If using a muffin pan, reduce the cooking time to about 20 minutes, testing to see if the rolls are done by pushing a metal skewer into the center of one of them to check it comes out clean.

nutty brown soda bread

Irish soda breads are not just quick and simple to make, they are also very satisfying to eat and make an excellent alternative to traditional yeast breads. This loaf has nuts kneaded into the dough for extra crunch and although it doesn't keep well, it does make great toast and can be frozen.

MAKES: I loaf

BAKING TIME: 35–40 minutes

2¾ cups (12 oz) plain white flour, plus extra for dusting

2 cups (8 oz) whole wheat plain flour

2 Tbsp butter

½ cup chopped almonds

⅓ cup raisins

2 Tbsp light brown muscovado sugar

1½ tsp baking soda

2½ cups buttermilk or plain yogurt

1 Preheat the oven to 375°F. In a mixing bowl, stir together the white flour and whole wheat flour. Rub in the butter and then stir in the almonds, raisins, brown sugar and baking soda.

2 Make a well in the center of the dry ingredients and pour in the buttermilk or yogurt. Stir in with a large metal spoon and then bring the dough together with your hands – dust them with flour first – and knead the dough until it is smooth. Alternatively it can be made in an electric mixer with a dough hook fitted.

3 Shape the dough into a ball about 8 inches across and place on a nonstick baking sheet. Cut a deep cross in the top of the loaf with a floured knife to allow air to get into the loaf as it bakes, and dust the top with flour.

4 Bake for 35–40 minutes or until the base sounds hollow when tapped. Transfer the loaf to a wire rack, cover with a clean kitchen towel and leave to cool before slicing and eating.

DID YOU KNOW?

Soda bread was first made in Ireland during the 1840s when baking soda became available to bakers there. Traditionally loaves are made with ordinary flour rather than strong bread flour, plus buttermilk and salt.

potato farls

The name 'farl' comes from the Gaelic word meaning 'four parts' and these griddled triangles of potato bread are a good way of using up leftover mashed potatoes. They make the best accompaniment there is to a traditional Irish fried breakfast but you can also spread them with butter and enjoy them just on their own. They are best eaten warm straight from the pan.

MAKES: 8 farls

COOKING TIME: about 20 minutes

2 Tbsp butter

4 cups cold mashed potatoes

¾ cup (4 oz) plain flour, plus extra for kneading

salt and pepper, to taste

1 Melt the butter and add the mashed potatoes. Stir in the flour until evenly combined and season with salt and pepper.

2 Transfer the mixture to a floured surface and knead until smooth. Divide it in half and roll or press out each half to a disk measuring about 9 inches in diameter. Cut each disk into 4 quarters.

3 Heat a nonstick skillet or griddle until hot and cook the potato farls in batches over a medium heat for 3–4 minutes on each side or until browned. Remove each batch from the pan and keep warm while you cook the remaining farls. Serve warm.

gluten-free breads

If you know someone who has to omit gluten from their diet, show them they no longer need miss out when the bread basket comes round. With gluten-free flours and baking powder, plus buckwheat flour and bran widely available, we prove you can make delicious breads that everyone will enjoy whether they follow a gluten-free diet or not.

gluten-free green olive and chorizo loaf

If you need to avoid gluten in your diet but don't want to give up bread, the good news is you can still enjoy it thanks to gluten-free flours becoming more widely available from supermarkets as well as health food shops. When buying baking powder to make this loaf, check the pack to ensure that it is gluten-free too, as not all baking powders are. As the dough is wet and similar to a thick batter, I'd recommend using an electric mixer rather than mixing it by hand.

SERVES: 8

BAKING TIME: 50 minutes

1⅓ cups (8 oz) gluten-free white bread flour

1 Tbsp gluten-free baking powder

1 tsp salt

1¼ cups buttermilk

3 eggs, beaten

2 Tbsp olive oil, plus extra for greasing

2 oz cured chorizo, finely diced

¼ cup pitted green olives, sliced

2 Tbsp grated Parmesan cheese

1 Preheat the oven to 350°F. Sift the flour, baking powder and salt into the bowl of an electric mixer fitted with a dough hook, add the buttermilk, eggs and olive oil and beat to make a smooth batter.

2 Add the chorizo, olives and 1 Tbsp Parmesan. Pour the batter into a greased 9- x 5-inch loaf pan lined with parchment paper and sprinkle with the remaining Parmesan.

3 Bake for 50 minutes or until a skewer pushed into the center of the loaf comes out clean. Cool in the pan for 5 minutes before turning out onto a wire rack.

raisin and flaxseed loaf

Flaxseeds are a powerhouse of nutrients so make an excellent addition to a bread dough. They need soaking, preferably overnight, before they are mixed with the other ingredients and any flaxseeds that are leftover should be stored in an airtight container in the fridge to keep them fresh. The dough is very sticky and quite difficult to work with if you mix it by hand but it does result in a deliciously moist loaf.

MAKES: I loaf

BAKING TIME: 35–40 minutes

¼ cup flaxseeds

about 2 cups (9 oz) gluten-free flour, plus extra for dusting the loaf pan

I Tbsp quick-rise dried yeast

I Tbsp bran

I tsp salt

I cup warm milk

½ cup plus 2 Tbsp corn syrup

I Tbsp canola oil, plus extra for greasing

½ cup raisins

1 Put the flaxseeds in a bowl, pour over enough water to cover them and leave overnight to swell. Drain the flaxseeds thoroughly and discard the soaking water.

2 Mix the flour, yeast, bran and salt together in a large bowl. Beat together the milk, corn syrup and canola oil and add to the flour mixture, along with the drained flaxseeds. Work everything together with your hand, a wooden spoon or a hand-held electric mixer on low speed until all the ingredients are thoroughly combined and you have a sticky dough.

3 Grease a 9- x 5-inch loaf pan with oil and dust with flour. Pour in the dough, scraping out any residue that sticks to the bowl. Smooth the surface of the dough with a floured knife, cover the pan with a damp kitchen towel and leave it to rise in a warm place for 30–45 minutes or until doubled in size.

4 Preheat the oven to 400°F, set the pan on the baking sheet on a low shelf in the oven and bake for 30 minutes or until the loaf sounds hollow when tapped on the base.

5 Turn out the loaf and wrap it in a dry kitchen towel. Leave it to cool on a wire rack.

buckwheat bread

Despite its name, buckwheat is not a type of wheat or cereal grain but the seed of a fruit related to rhubarb, making it gluten free and therefore a suitable alternative for anyone who has to avoid wheat in their diet. Packed with nutrients, including a high level of magnesium to keep our blood flowing smoothly through our veins, buckwheat is also linked to helping to lower cholesterol and blood pressure.

MAKES: I loaf

BAKING TIME: 35–40 minutes

2 egg yolks

4 Tbsp very soft butterx

3–4 Tbsp granulated sugar (see Tip)

I cup (4½ oz) buckwheat flour, plus extra for dusting

2 tsp gluten-free baking powder

½ tsp salt

⅔ cup milk

3 Tbsp applesauce

2 egg whites

oil, for greasing

1 Preheat the oven to 400°F.

2 In a mixing bowl, whisk the egg yolks, butter and sugar together until light and creamy. Stir in the buckwheat flour, baking powder and salt.

3 Whisk together the milk and applesauce and stir into the buckwheat mixture.

4 Whisk the egg whites in another bowl until they hold stiff but not dry peaks. Stir I Tbsp of the whisked egg whites into the buckwheat mixture to lighten it before carefully folding in the rest with a large metal spoon.

5 Grease a 9-inch square pan and dust it with buckwheat. Set the pan on a baking sheet and pour in the batter, spreading the top level with a floured knife.

6 Bake for 35–40 minutes or until a metal skewer pushed into the center of the loaf comes out clean. Cool for 10 minutes in the pan before turning out the loaf onto a wire rack and leaving it to cool completely.

TIP If using sweetened applesauce, only add 3 Tbsp sugar to the batter. When adding the whisked egg whites to the batter, stir in 1 Tbsp to begin with to lighten the batter and make it easier to fold in the remainder. Do this folding carefully with a large metal spoon and using a figure-eight movement so as not to knock out all the air you've just whisked into the whites.

baking notes

baking notes

baking notes

troubleshooting

BADLY RISEN LOAF? POOR TEXTURE? CRACKED CRUST?.....WHAT WENT WRONG?

The dough hasn't risen as much as it should have in the oven

- Yeast was stale so not sufficiently active.
- Liquid was too warm so it killed the yeast.
- Dough over-proved so loaf collapsed in the oven.
- Too much salt and/or sugar mixed into the dough.
- The dough was risen and/or proved for too short a time.
- Not enough liquid added to the dough making it too dry.

The loaf has a poor texture

- A heavy, close texture results from using too soft a flour or adding too much salt.
- Dough was insufficiently kneaded.
- A coarse, uneven texture with large holes results if the dough was not knocked down properly or it was left uncovered during rising.
- Too much liquid will result in a coarse dough, as will over-proving.

The loaf has a cracked crust or 'flying top'

- The dough was under-proved.
- The top dried out during proving.
- Oven was too hot.
- Slashing the top of the dough before the loaf is baked helps prevent a 'flying top' (also known as oven-spring).

The loaf has a sour, yeasty flavor and smells of alcohol

- Dough was over-proved or risen for too long and at too high a temperature.
- Too much yeast added to the dough.
- Yeast was stale.

cup conversions

AMERICAN	IMPERIAL	METRIC
1 cup flour	5oz	150g
1 cup caster / granulated sugar	8oz	225g
1 cup brown sugar	6oz	175g
1 cup butter/margarine/lard	8oz	225g
1 cup sultanas / raisins	7oz	200g
1 cup currants	5oz	150g
1 cup graound almonds	4oz	110g
1 cup gloden syrup	12oz	350g
1 cup uncooked rice	7oz	200g
1 cup grated cheese	4oz	110g
1 stick butter	4oz	110g

liquid conversions

AMERICAN	IMPERIAL	METRIC
1 tbsp	½ fl oz	15ml
⅛ cup	1 fl oz	30ml
¼ cup	2 fl oz	60ml
½ cup	4 fl oz	120ml
1 cup	8 fl oz	240ml
1 pint	16 fl oz	480ml

index

photography credits

Ian Garlick: pages 41, 47, 53, 57, 67, 75, 85, 96, 116, 119, 133, 145, 149, 153, 159, 163, 172, 175, 195, 216, 224, 226, 233

Stockfood: pages 68, 71, 99, 100, 126, 191, 206

Other photography courtesy of iStockphoto and Shutterstock

Every effort has been made to credit photographers and copyright-holders. If any have been overlooked, Pulp Media will be pleased to make the necessary corrections in subsequent editions and on their website www.pulp.me.com